Attitudes
in Teaching and Education

William Hare

Detselig Enterprises Ltd.

Calgary, Alberta

Canadian Cataloguing in Publication Data

Hare, William.
Attitudes in teaching and education

ISBN 1-55059-067-7

1. Education – Philosophy.   2. Teaching
3. Teachers – Attitudes.   4. Discrimination
in education.   I. Title.
LB1025.3.H37   1993   370'.1   C93-091409-0

Detselig Enterprises Ltd.
210, 1220 Kensington Rd. N.W.
Calgary, Alberta T2N 3P5

This title is available in the U.S. from: Temeron Books Inc.,
P.O. Box 896, Bellingham, Washington 98227.

Printed in Canada   SAN 115-0324   ISBN 1-55059-067-7

To my son, Antony,
whose expertise with computers has been invaluable.

Other books by William Hare:

Open-mindedness and Education

In Defence of Open-mindedness

Controversies in Teaching

Philosophy of Education: Introductory Readings (with John P. Portelli)

Reason in Teaching and Education

What Makes A Good Teacher

What To Do? Case Studies for Teachers (with John P. Portelli)

Contents

Financial support provided by the Alberta Foundation for the Arts, a beneficiary of the Lottery Fund of the Government of Alberta and from the Department of Communications.

Preface and Acknowledgments

This collection brings together ten papers I have published in recent years. I am grateful to the editors and publishers of the journals and books in which they originally appeared for permission to reprint. The details are cited below. Earlier versions of these papers were presented to audiences at Guelph University, McMaster University, University of Sydney, Australia, McGill University, Dalhousie University, and Saint Mary's University, on which occasions I received many helpful comments.

The essays fall into four groups, the first of which is historical in character. Chapter one traces the emergence of philosophy of education in Canada during the twentieth century; and chapter two reviews the important but now somewhat neglected work of Bertrand Russell on the philosophy of education. The second group, chapters three, four, and five, comprises three discussions of open-mindedness which extend the work I have done earlier on this topic in my books on open-mindedness by applying the idea in various contexts. In the third group, some questions dealing with propaganda and bias are considered. Chapter six reviews a notorious Canadian case in which a teacher was ultimately dismissed because his lessons amounted to a program of indoctrination; chapter seven illustrates how difficult it is to avoid simplistic rules entering into guidelines drawn up for teachers anxious to avoid bias. The final group consists of three essays which deal with some philosophical issues in the context of teaching. Chapter eight asks how we are to conceive of teaching and what kinds of ideals and attitudes are appropriate for teachers. Chapter nine examines some popular slogans about teaching which have attracted attention in recent years. And chapter ten illustrates how a teacher might introduce a philosophical dimension to the classroom, drawing on Plato's *Apology*.

Work on these topics, especially on Russell's views on teaching and on the Keegstra case, has convinced me that the ideals which Russell defended are sadly neglected in the Canadian context, and I have addressed the question of the moral, intellectual, and personal qualities which teachers need in a recent book, *What Makes A Good Teacher* (1993), to which the reader is referred.

Publication details for each chapter are as follows: 1. *Eidos* 10, 1, 1991; 2. *Russell* 7, 1, 1987; 3. *Journal of Philosophy of Education* 19, 2, 1985; 4. *Journal of Moral Education* 16, 2, 1987; 5. *Ethics in Education* 7, 3, 1988; 6. *Canadian Journal of Education* 15, 4, 1990; 7. *Journal of Applied Philosophy* 2, 1, 1985; 8. Evelina Miranda and Romulo Magsino (eds.), *Teaching, Schools and Society* Falmer Press, 1990; 9. *International Review of Education* 36, 1, 1986; 10. *The Classical World* 80, 1, 1986.

1
Philosophy of Education in Canada

Philosophy of education has a long and interesting history in Canada though it is only recently that strong links have been formed with general philosophy. In the second half of the century, a new rigor came into philosophy of education as a result of developments in the United States in the 1940s and 1950s, and these changes started to take hold in Canada in the 1960s. Today, philosophy of education is a lively and productive branch of philosophy in this country.

The Early Years

In a paper on liberal education published in 1960, the late James Paton concluded his discussion with the following plea:

> I would like to see at least one university department of philosophy in Canada capable of winning the respect of philosophers everywhere, but which would not cut itself off from our colleges of education whose job it is, in their teaching of educational theory, to build bridges between the abstract ideas of the academic thinker and the practical realities of the classroom.[1]

The complaint implicit here, from a keen observer of Canadian education, is one which could not plausibly be made today. In the meantime, of course, the colleges of education have been integrated within the universities in Canada.[2] What needs to be emphasized, however, is that the links between general philosophy[3] and the philosophy of education have been immeasurably strengthened in the intervening thirty years. Philosophy of education in Canada continues to be taught mainly, but by no means exclusively, in faculties, schools, and departments of education in the universities, but this institutional reality is not a reflection of completely separate lives at the level of inquiry. There has indeed been a dramatic rapprochement in the years since Paton's comment gave timely impetus to a movement already underway. Looking back, we can see that things were changing or about to change just as the plea was being made.

Let us be clear at the outset, however, that it would be nonsense to conclude that philosophical reflection on education was non-existent in Canada prior to the 1960s. Indeed, at the turn of the century, one finds philosophers writing about education. For example, Samuel Walters Dyde (1862-1947), professor of mental philosophy at Queen's University from 1889-1911, argued in a 1904 paper for openness and humility of mind as essential aspects of the educated person.[4] The suspicion that such writing would be no more than the mere statement of "high-level directives" is simply not borne out on inspection.[5] Dyde set out to clarify what these aims involve and to distinguish them carefully from other attitudes with which they are often confused. He clearly saw himself writing in a tradition of philosophical commentary on education, his immediate inspiration being Newman, with references also to Socrates and Plato.

Coming somewhat closer to our own day, even a cursory account would be inadequate without mention of Rupert C. Lodge (1886-1961), a member of the philosophy department at the University of Manitoba from 1916-47, who wrote a book and various papers on philosophy of education which were widely known.[6] It is too easy, I think, to dismiss Lodge as merely parading a variety of isms from which educational prescriptions might be drawn, a move which only encourages the view that philosophers of education of the later analytic period were doing something altogether different from their predecessors. A more sympathetic view might see Lodge constructing and reviewing various models of education in the manner of Scheffler on teaching. John Macdonald (1888-1972), professor of philosophy at the University of Alberta from 1921-52, also produced a number of books and articles in philosophy of education. Macdonald saw philosophy of education as a practical application of philosophy, but cautioned against doctrinairism where one set of principles is regarded as ultimate truth.[7]

A significant contribution was also made by numerous individuals who were not trained philosophers. Neville V. Scarfe (1908-88), who was Dean of Education at the University of British Columbia from 1956-72, wrote in a philosophical vein about the aims of education and other subjects.[8] Scarfe's own background was in geography but he was influenced by Percy Nunn at the University of London in the 1930s, and we might say of Scarfe without prejudice, what Brian Hill has said of Nunn himself, that he exemplified a tradition of scholarly amateurism.[9] His emphasis on the individual in education was very much influenced by Nunn. R. S. K. Seeley (1908-57), approaching education from a background in classics, gave an interesting set of lectures in 1947 which explored some philosophical questions about the nature of university education, a topic which has continued to be of considerable interest in Canada.[10] And there were many, like my late colleague at Dalhousie University, Alex S. Mowat (1905-84), also a classicist, who raised critical questions about the achievement of progressive education.[11] There is, in fact, a considerable body of now much neglected work which, it is to be hoped, will in time be reviewed and assessed.[12] That investigation, if it is to be adequate, will have to look at the character of the work done and not limit its scope to the work of "professional" philosophers of education.

A Turning Point

Having said this, however, and acknowledging too that recent philosophy of education has tended to underestimate, even disparage, the contributions of the writers in the early part of the century, it is also true, I believe, that a new rigor and sophistication came into philosophy of education in the second half of the century,[13] as new developments in philosophy were appreciated and utilized. Originating primarily in the United States in the 1940s, with honorable exceptions elsewhere, new standards of excellence were to be set for philosophy of education as closer ties with general philosophy were forged. Certainly, the story would have to include the formation of the Philosophy of Education Society in the United States in 1941, and the founding of the journal *Educational Theory* in 1951, developments which were to give philosophers of education in that country a greater sense of identity and a forum.[14] These developments were to culminate in the great debate about the nature and purpose of philosophy of education in the early 1950s, the main contributions to which can now be conveniently found in the collection *What is the Philosophy of Education?*[15] That debate brought distinguished philosophers such as Susanne K. Langer, Sidney Hook, William K. Frankena, Max Black, and Abraham Edel into spirited exchanges with philosophers of education of the calibre of Harry S. Broudy and Kingsley Price and the result could not but be beneficial for the discipline. In 1960, Israel Scheffler produced *The Language of Education*, a book which was to secure his reputation as the senior philosopher of education in North America and represent a new standard for others.

As late as 1963, however, Andrew F. Skinner concluded that philosophy of education was comparatively neglected in Canada, with faculties of education and teachers' colleges giving pride of place to methods classes and supervised teaching.[16] Another piece of evidence with respect to the comparative neglect of the subject comes from the reviews conducted by Willard Brehaut of graduate theses in education in Canadian universities in the period 1956-61.[17] Brehaut found only five theses dealing with philosophical issues out of a total of nearly three hundred theses completed in this five year period. In retrospect, however, it now seems that the early 1960s was just about the last moment when such pessimistic reports could be made.[18] It is, I think, foolish to try to place an exact date on changing attitudes or on emerging disciplines and conceptions of disciplines, but by the end of the decade the picture had drastically altered.

A major turning point, surely, was the International Seminar on Philosophy and Education held at the Ontario Institute for Studies in Education in March 1966.[19] Five philosophers of education, including R. S. Peters, presented papers which were commented on mainly by philosophers then with the department of philosophy at the University of Toronto.[20] In June 1968, a conference on moral education was held in Toronto, again sponsored by OISE, which brought philosophers, philosophers of education, and psychologists together. This meeting of philosophers and psychologists reflected the emerging differentiation within educational theory, but also indicated that educational theory involves an interdisciplinary conversation.[21] In the Fall term of the same year, R. M. Hare gave two public lectures on moral education at OISE, and later was to give a course of lectures on his ethical theory.[22] And in 1970, OISE hosted a conference on "New directions in philosophy of education," which was attended by many of the major figures in philosophy of education in North America, including Scheffler.[23] None of the leading British writers attended.

There were, of course, related developments elsewhere in Canada during the 1960s. Perhaps the most significant was the appointment across the country in various universities of scholars with strong academic credentials and experience in philosophy of education. Notable appointments included Charles Brauner, Jerrold Coombs, Murray Elliott, and Roi Daniels at the University of British Columbia, Gordon Eastwood and Nirmal Battacharya at the University of Alberta, Tasos Kazepides at Simon Fraser University, and Harold Entwistle at what was Sir George Williams University (now Concordia). There was an active Northwest Philosophy of Education Society, a regional branch of the American PES, and its conference held in Vancouver in 1969 was to result in a special issue of the *Journal of Education* (UBC) in 1971, edited by Roi Daniels, concerned with rights and respect for persons in education. Moreover, in the late 1960s, major educational reports were being produced in Canada which prompted considerable discussion across the country and to which philosophers of education contributed.[24] By the end of the decade, there was considerable evidence that philosophy of education in Canada had become a very active branch of philosophical inquiry and a distinctive voice in educational theory.[25]

If we turn for the moment to the situation today, it is worth noting, first, that a considerable number of philosophers in Canada who work in departments of philosophy, and whose philosophical interests may be wide-ranging, take a serious interest in philosophy of education as an aspect of philosophical inquiry. One thinks immediately of Rodger Beehler, Anthony Blair, Robert Carter, Wesley Cragg, Brian Hendley, Katherine Morgan, and Jay Newman.[26] The example of Israel Scheffler and Richard Peters in particular has been a powerful influence in creating a new climate of opinion in the past quarter century which has seen philosophy of education re-emerge as a reputable area of philosophical inquiry.[27] Both Scheffler and Peters began their careers in general philosophy and had produced excellent articles and books in philosophy before making philosophy of education central in their own research and teaching. This happened in both cases during the 1950s, Scheffler somewhat earlier than Peters, as the analytic approach in general philosophy came to be applied to educational theory.[28] Scheffler and Peters may be seen as reflecting in their practice the view advanced in 1953 by the Committee on the nature and function of the discipline of philosophy of education, that philosophy of education is part of the general enterprise of philosophy distinguished from other areas of philosophy by the subject matter to which its attention is directed.[29] The Canadian philosophers mentioned are, of course, followers of Scheffler and Peters only in the sense that they have followed them in thinking of education as an area worthy of serious philosophical consideration. It is, I think, all to the good to have members of departments of philosophy including philosophy of education as part of their range.

Complementing the first point, but even more significant, is the fact that philosophers of education in Canada today, again following the lead of Scheffler, Peters, Passmore and others, typically have a strong preparation in general philosophy. They are, in fact, competent philosophers whose *primary* interest happens to be in philosophy of education rather than, say, philosophy of science or ethics, though it is not unusual to find them doing work from time to time in other areas of philosophy. It is clear now to all that philosophy of education cannot really flourish if it is divorced from developments in general philosophy, if its practitioners are themselves out of touch with what is happening in areas of philosophy on which the philosophy of education necessarily draws. Equally clearly, philosophers of education need constant interaction with the field of education, with teachers, schools, curricula, and so on, if they are to avoid the trap Scheffler was at pains to point out of thinking that philosophical skills can be applied mechanically to educational problems. Scheffler called for judgment, tact, intelligence, and wisdom.[30]

Despite the general cutbacks which occurred in the 1980s, philosophy of education is holding its own. Across Canada, one or more philosophers of education can be found at virtually every university. It is this community, the philosophers of education working primarily in faculties of education, which constitutes the core of philosophy of education in Canada. My impression is that, on the whole, Canadian philosophers of education take the view, championed of late by Jonas Soltis, that philosophy of education ought to reach out to practitioners in what Soltis calls an attempt to make the educational enterprise as rationally self-reflective as possible. They would be less inclined to endorse the purist view, defended by Harvey Siegel and others, that the production of philosophical insight alone is what matters, regardless of considerations of relevance.[31] In this, at least, Canadians would follow the view of R. S. Peters, as stated in his general editor's note included in the various volumes in the International Library of the Philosophy of Education, that the discipline has to be both practically relevant and philosophically competent.

By the early 1970s, philosophers of education were active on the national scene. A glance, for example, at the program for the Annual Conference of the Canadian Society for the Study of Education held at Queen's University in May 1973 will reveal the names of a dozen or so philosophers of education, including Don Cochrane, Roi Daniels, Murray Elliott, Michael Jackson, Joe Malikail and myself. A high level of activity has been sustained over the years at the annual meetings, and led in 1976 to the formation of the Canadian Philosophy of Education Society which now numbers about one hundred members.[32] The decision was taken at the annual meeting in 1986 to establish a journal, and the first issue of *Paideusis: Journal of the Canadian Philosophy of Education Society* appeared in the Fall of 1987 under the editorship of Paul O'Leary. In his opening editorial, he remarked that the journal would not function as a closed shop in which only those who are "certified" philosophers of education can work, thus keeping the lines of communication open. Women philosophers have played a central role in the membership and executive of CPES, as mention of such names as Maryann Ayim, Sharon Bailin, and Olga McKenna will confirm, and women have been active and influential contributors to the literature, as we shall see.

It is not uncommon to hear it said that Canadian philosophers of education, especially in the 1970s, were following something popularly known as the "London line," a phrase meant to suggest that the work and ideas of R. S. Peters at the University of London dominated the approach taken in philosophy of education in this country.[33] Certainly, Peters' work was well known and the subject of considerable discussion, and some did, and still do, follow him closely.[34] The idea, however, that our work in Canada was mainly inspired by, let alone dominated by, Richard Peters is simply not supported by the evidence. This, I should say, is the case whether we have in mind substantive, attitudinal, or methodological influences, and also more general conceptions of the philosopher's sphere of activity.

Consider, first, the work done in Canada on moral education in the period following the renewed interest in philosophy of education, an area which has proved to be one of the busiest.[35] Peters had written on this topic since the early 1960s, and it would not have been surprising to have seen his influence. It was not his ideas, however, but those of Lawrence Kohlberg which commanded most attention. Kohlberg's stage theory of development, and his concerns about relativism, indoctrination, and justice constituted a large part of the agenda which inspired and provoked Canadian philosophers of education. In the wake of the Mackay Report (1969), Crittenden wrote a monograph in which the ideas of Kohlberg were subjected to detailed criticism and in which Crittenden argued against a preoccupation with moral reasoning to the exclusion of moral content. There is no noticeable influence from Peters either in substance or approach.[36] Kohlberg also loomed large in the various writings of Clive Beck on moral education, but Beck had his own distinctive ethical theory to apply and was more influenced by Morris Ginsberg than R. S. Peters. Beck also took his ideas into the schools with his Moral Education Project in Pickering starting in 1969, a practical engagement which enlarged the sphere of the philosopher beyond that envisaged by Peters.[37] This kind of school based project is also witnessed in the work of the Association for Values Education and Research (AVER) which included a number of philosophers of education at UBC.[38] Kohlberg's influence is also seen clearly in the approach to values education in the AVER schoolwork.

Consider also Peters' conception of education in which a central strand was the idea that education is intrinsically valuable, a point which was underlined by the alleged ordinary language differences between training and education. This paradigm of analysis, however, was already in 1970 failing to command complete support in Canada where, for example, Harold Entwistle rejected "the conventional wisdom that education has no concern with those activities which have utilitarian or instrumental values and which appear to lack intrinsic justification."[39] He wrote sympathetically about vocational education at a time when a certain conception of liberal education, sharply contrasted with vocational training, was riding high. Entwistle published a second book in 1970 dealing with child-centred theories of education which again demonstrated his independent position. Among other things, we find a more generous reading of the earlier writers such as Dewey and Whitehead than was to be found in Peters at this time. Whereas Peters had portrayed Whitehead as "enunciating values," Entwistle rightly characterized Whitehead's principle of rhythm as a valuable conceptual tool.[40] There was to be no truck with the idea that philosophy of education had sprung into existence fully formed circa 1960.

One reason why some Canadian philosophers of education did not look to Peters for guidance was that Peters' view was itself not always well understood, with the result that many were no more charitable towards Peters than he had been to earlier philosophers of education. Peters, it is true, had tended to emphasize the ordinary language approach to analytical philosophy rather more than Scheffler and this, coupled with the fact that, at his major appearance in Canada at the 1966 Toronto conference, he had opted to restrict his attention to conceptual questions related to the aims of education, led to his general position being somewhat misinterpreted. Particularly problematic was the comment in his inaugural lecture that "conceptual clarification is preeminently the task of a philosopher of education."[41] Did this mean that conceptual clarification was the preeminent task? Or that philosophers were preeminently suited to this important but limited work? Many were inclined to take the former reading and, given his ordinary language approach, drifted into the idea that Peters was "playing with words." Of course, nine of the eleven chapters in Peters' *Ethics and Education* (1966) were devoted to questions of ethical *justification,* and Peters stressed in the Introduction to this book that conceptual analysis had to be linked to the justification of beliefs, but it is surprising what one can fail to notice once a particular view has set in. The result is that many turned their backs on Peters believing that he represented a more limited conception of philosophy of education than was in fact the case.

One further point is in order concerning the matter of general influences. We need to remember that in drawing closer to general philosophy, philosophers of education do not encounter a single tradition. Philosophy itself, at any particular time, presents a variety of approaches. If some looked to Peters, others looked to Sartre for inspiration. Existentialism has had a continuing attraction for philosophers of education, including George Kneller and Maxine Greene in the United States, and in Canada Laurence Stott wrote a series of papers drawing on and applying the ideas and insights of Sartre.[42] In a review of philosophy of education in Britain in 1982, R. F. Dearden commented that no one had been convinced there that phenomenology represented a fruitful approach.[43] In Canada, however, it is clear that Max van Manen has found it a fruitful approach, and has demonstrated this in a spate of publications over the years.[44] Again the point is that philosophy does not take a single form even if certain approaches predominate at times, and there is much to be gained by reaching out to other perspectives.

Recent Work

The last two decades have been productive ones for philosophy of education in Canada. There has been activity on a great variety of fronts leading to a diverse body of publications which includes: several introductory, yet innovative, books on philosophy of education, a number of general collections of essays, special issues of journals and yearbooks, a journal devoted to the subject now in its sixth year, a dictionary of educational concepts, a score or more of books on specialized topics, and what must be hundreds of articles in national and international journals.[45] The subjects covered have been equally diverse and include virtually the whole range of topics addressed in the field. Naturally, local and national issues have often given this work a Canadian flavor, but these are dealt with so as to bring out the fundamental questions which they raise. A notable example here would be Don Cochrane's critique of an infamous curriculum report in Saskatchewan in 1984 around which he compiled a collection of essays.[46] The brouhaha surrounding this episode put to rest the idea that philosophy of education was confined to the ivory tower.

One major focus in recent books on philosophy of education in Canada has been the detailed study of particular educational aims. Peters had, of course, discussed the nature of educational aims and had developed a general conception of education, but did not explore the nature and value of specific aims in any detail. In 1981, John McPeck published *Critical Thinking and Education,* in which he argued against the fashionable conception of critical thinking as a general skill, taking the view that critical thinking was subject and context dependent.[47] This book, and McPeck's arguments, have been centre-stage in the philosophical debate about critical thinking which is on-going. Sharon Bailin addressed another perennial aim of education in a book which argued that creativity is a matter of achieving extraordinary ends and which rejected many fashionable views about creativity, such as the idea that rules and skills inhibit creativity.[48] Bailin's reminder that creativity has to do with significant achievements constitutes a welcome philosophical challenge to the ever-present tender-mindedness in contemporary education which pictures creativity as utterly subjective and beyond assessment. Eamonn Callan's *Autonomy and Schooling* (1988) made a substantial contribution to the literature on autonomy as an aim of education, an area which has been of considerable interest since Dearden's pioneering efforts in the early 1970s.[49] Callan argued for the development of autonomous persons who are characterized by a high degree of realism and independence of mind. My own work on open-mindedness also falls into this general category of specific educational aims. I have characterized open-mindedness as a willingness to form and revise one's views in the light of evidence and argument, have argued for the significance of this in a variety of educational contexts, and have defended this ideal against a host of objections.[50] These four aims, critical thinking, creativity, autonomy, and open-mindedness, connect at various points and exist within a wider network of educational aims, but we await a comprehensive account which would situate them in an overall account of education.

A second area where interesting work has been done concerns critical commentary on particular authors. The best example here is Brian Hendley's examination of Dewey, Russell, and Whitehead in a book which has done much to overturn the unfortunate view that the earlier writers were not really philosophers of education at all.[51] And in looking at the practical involvement of these individuals in education, Hendley has commented effectively on the limitations of philosophy of education conducted in isolation from concrete reality. I would add, however, that the point could have been made without condemning analytic philosophy of education as ultimately futile, an exaggeration which might undermine Hendley's commendable concern to keep the philosophical conversation open to a variety of approaches.[52] A second notable example of this genre is Harold Entwistle's study of Antonio Gramsci in which he set out to resolve the "apparent contradiction between his revolutionary political and social theory and his emphasis upon the value of traditional educational practice with reference to the content and processes of schooling."[53] Entwistle's critical analysis shows that Gramsci has been more often quoted than studied by radical educational theorists, and predictably efforts have been made to marginalize his interpretation.[54] What passes for criticism in such efforts is no more than the fixing of tired and tiresome labels (reductionist, undialectical, ahistorical), against which fashionable power-play Entwistle's own work is a very useful antidote. Anyone interested in the difference between philosophical argument and ideology mongering need go no further. Finally in this area of work, one might mention the special issue of *Paideusis* in 1990 on the ideas of John Henry Newman.[55]

Canadian philosophers of education have also produced several books in recent years dealing with curriculum, schools, and teaching. In his *Giving Teaching Back to Teachers* (1984), Robin Barrow launched a blistering attack on many of the fashionable assumptions which influence curriculum theory today, especially perhaps the idea that curriculum design is an applied science, the false sense of precision and expertise which pervades the field, the search for teacher-proof materials, the neglect of particular circumstances which demand insight and judgment on the part of teachers, and the spurious nature of alleged rules of teaching.[56] Teaching is given back to teachers when it is recognized that "the judgment of the individual teacher . . . must be paramount in deciding how to proceed, rather than the generalized demands of some curriculum design or otherwise imposed rules of educational experts" (p. 264).

In *Better Schools: A Values Perspective* (1990), Clive Beck outlined a "manifesto" which includes: the need for school and society to work together, the promotion of human well being, more attention to values, culture, religion, politics, economics, and ecology, the abandonment of neutrality in teaching, attention to the atmosphere of the school, and a common curriculum in non-selective schools with heterogeneous classes.[57] Many of these sometimes controversial themes have been emerging in philosophy of education over the past decade, and it is to Beck's credit to have brought them together in an overall view. It is an example of philosophy of education returning to what Hendley calls the traditional task of general theory building but at the same time making those conceptual distinctions and observations which are vital to the task.

Alan Pearson has discussed the ever-present theory/practice debate in teacher education in his book *The Teacher* (1989).[58] Inspired by Alasdair MacIntyre, Pearson considered the idea of teaching as a practice which involves standards of excellence, obedience to rules, and the achievement of goods. Building on these claims, Pearson distinguished various kinds of knowledge a teacher needs to employ: causal, normative, experiential, subject matter, and general knowledge; and he discussed the complexities involved in utilizing such knowledge to formulate intentions and plans. An account is developed of the relationship between theory and practice in teacher education based on a conception of teaching as an intentional activity, dependent on knowledge, where the inevitable complexities which arise require revision of plans, beliefs, and intentions.

A final area which needs to be mentioned in this necessarily brief and partial survey concerns feminism and women's issues in the context of education. Debra Shogan's work stems from the challenging ideas introduced in the early 1980s by Carol Gilligan and Nel Noddings which centred on caring as an orientation in ethics by contrast with a justice conception. Shogan, however, has disputed the emerging dichotomy of care versus justice while maintaining that caring is central to morality.[59] Her book explores the conception of a caring person as one who desires the welfare *and* fair treatment of other people. A symposium published in 1985 on gender-free public schooling featured three Canadian philosophers of education, Maryann Ayim, Kathryn Morgan, and Barbara Houston.[60] Ayim subjected various arguments for the traditional, essentially male-privileged view to critical analysis; Morgan argued for the complete elimination of gender as a social category; and Houston defended a gender-sensitive approach, understood as one which eliminates gender-bias. All three have written extensively on issues such as sexism and sex-role stereotyping, androgyny as an aim in education, gender as a factor in employment opportunities and income levels, and women's rights.

Occasionally, though not all that often, one encounters references in Canadian philosophy of education to Derrida, Foucault, and other so-called postmodern writers, but such references tend to incorporate insights derived from these authors rather than constitute any kind of fundamental paradigm shift. There has been no great enthusiasm for extreme theses sometimes associated with these writers which seek to reduce all knowledge to ideology or power. Rather one finds a willingness to draw on discussions of these and other concepts when they can illuminate particular aspects of philosophical problems.[61] There *are* insights to be found, but interspersed with a great deal of vagueness and rhetoric. The lessons learned in the recent past about slogans in education are still relevant. It is also worth noting that the insights often amount to reminders, though this is not to lessen their significance. If deconstruction, for example, involves showing how a concept has been ideologically or culturally constructed, that activity is a valuable aspect of philosophy and may have been neglected at times, but it is surely not new in philosophy or philosophy of education.

Concluding Comment

We have seen how difficult it was in the early 1960s to discern that an exciting period of growth was about to occur. Philosophy does not confer predictive ability, and one cannot say in what direction philosophy of education will go in this country nor how it will fare. I am also dubious about setting general agendas for the subject, since events which are unpredictable and beyond one's control can force problems onto the agenda or make certain issues less significant than they were. Dewey observed that philosophy tends to come after events as an *ex post facto* enterprise.[62] So we should be cautious ourselves before making confident pronouncements. Certainly, the economic climate and shortage of new openings gives one pause. The gains which have been made could be lost if positions are not filled when retirements occur. In a more positive vein, there are several centres across the country where doctoral work is undertaken in philosophy of education, and which attract excellent students. If the link between abstract ideas and practical realities which Paton envisaged is to be preserved and developed, graduates of these programs must find their way into teaching and research and help maintain philosophy of education as a vigorous element in Canadian education.[63]

Notes

1. J. M. Paton, "Liberal education: The teacher's prime concern," *The Canadian College of Teachers 3*, 1960: 5-23. This paper is reprinted in D. A. MacIver (ed.), *Concern and Competence in Canadian Education: Essays by J. M. Paton*, Toronto: Faculty of Education, 1973: 25-39. James Paton (1906-91) taught at what is now the Faculty of Education, University of Toronto, from 1963-72. For many years, he was the editor of *Teacher Education* and philosophy of education was well represented in its pages. I met him in the late 1960s and can personally testify to his supportive concern for younger scholars, and to his open-minded attitude towards new developments in philosophy of education.

2. With the exception of the Nova Scotia Teachers' College.

3. There is no easy way to draw the distinction, which I hope is clear enough, between philosophy of education and the general discipline of philosophy. One common formulation in terms of "pure" philosophy and philosophy of education is potentially misleading, not to mention question-begging. My point is simply that in recent

decades, the philosophy of education has become more integrated with the general activity of philosophy, to the point that it is a recognized member of the family. I shall also distinguish later between philosophers who include philosophy of education among their research and teaching activities, and philosophers of education who make that area their primary, sometimes exclusive, concern.

4. S. W. Dyde, "Should there be a faculty of education in the university?", *Queen's Quarterly 12*, 2, 1904: 165-77. Dyde was born in Ottawa, and studied at Queen's University taking degrees in classics and philosophy. He wrote on Hegel, translated parts of Plato, and published some verse. Much of the material in the early period of the century is to be found in the various university journals such as *Queen's Quarterly* and *Dalhousie Review*. It is to be hoped that the best of this "lost" material will be assembled in a collection which would represent the philosophy of education in Canada in the twentieth century.

5. I allude to the well known phrase which R. S. Peters used by way of dismissing what he thought passed for philosophy of education in the early part of the century. See his "The philosophy of education," in J. W. Tibble (ed.), *The Study of Education,* London: Routledge and Kegan Paul, 1966: 63.

6. Rupert C. Lodge, *Philosophy of Education*, New York: Harper, 1937. See also his essay "Philosophy and education," *Dalhousie Review 14*, 1934-5: 281-90.

7. John MacDonald, *Mind, School and Civilization: A Contribution to the Philosophy of Education*, Chicago: University of Chicago Press, 1952. Also *A Philosophy of Education,* Toronto: Gage, 1965. See also "Administration for what?", *Canadian Education 9*, 4, 1954: 63-75, where Macdonald attempts to relate philosophy to the problems faced by the educational administrator. Macdonald was with the University of Alberta from 1921 until his retirement in 1952, and joined the university when philosophy, psychology, and education formed a single department. From 1945-1952, he was Dean of Arts and Science.

8. See Neville V. Scarfe, *A Philosophy of Education: An Inaugural Lecture at the University of Manitoba*, Winnipeg: University of Manitoba Press, 1952. See also Scarfe's fine essay "The aims of education in a free society," reprinted in Anand Malik (ed.), *Social Foundations of Canadian Education*, Scarborough: Prentice-Hall, 1969: 7-26. Also his papers: "How good are our universities?", *Canadian Education 8*, 2, 1953: 3-16; "A philosophy of primary education," *Journal of Education (UBC) 6*, 1961: 46-52; and "The modern university," in *Canadian Education and Research Digest 4*, 2, 1964: 102-6. Scarfe also played an important role in building up philosophy of education at UBC in the 1960s. Also at UBC was Kenneth F. Argue who called for educators to participate in "this urgent task of clarifying our social ideals and, what is equally important, making them more explicit in Canadian ways of living." See his paper, "Some thoughts concerning the role of the educator in today's educational controversy," in *Thought* from The Learned Societies of Canada 1960, Toronto: Gage, 1960: 109-14.

9. Brian V. Hill, *Education and the Endangered Individual*, New York: Dell, 1973: 91. T. Percy Nunn (1870-1944) was a very competent and respected philosopher in the early years of the twentieth century. In 1920, he wrote *Education: Its Data and First Principles*, one of the most influential books on education in Britain between the wars.

10. R. S. K. Seeley, *The Function of the University*, Toronto: Oxford University Press, 1948. Seeley was Provost of Trinity College, University of Toronto. One paper drawing on his work is David A. Stewart, "Aims of a university education," *Dalhousie Review 29*, 1, 1950: 81-9. Note also the papers by Dyde and Scarfe (1953,

1964) referred to earlier as further evidence of a general interest in the question of university education, its nature, and aims, in Canada.

11. Alex S. Mowat, "How progressive are the 'progressives'?", *University of Toronto Quarterly 24*, 1, 1954: 26-33. Probably the best known of these critics was the historian Hilda Neatby (1904-75) who published *So Little for the Mind,* Toronto: Clarke, Irwin, 1953, and *A Temperate Dispute,* Toronto: Clarke, Irwin, 1954, books which are certainly part of the philosophical critique of education in Canada.

12. This early period in Canadian philosophy of education would make an admirable doctoral project.

13. I have noted elsewhere how the philosophers who wrote on education in the early part of the century, such as Russell, were entirely neglected when I was a graduate student in Britain and Canada in the late 1960s. I have also pointed to some continuities. See further chapter 2, this collection.

14. Other milestones included: (i) The publication of C. D. Hardie's book, *Truth and Fallacy in Educational Theory* in 1942. Hardie was at the University of Tasmania, and was influenced by analytic approaches to philosophy pioneered at Cambridge. It has become fashionable to speak of this book as having emerged still-born from the press, but D. J. O'Connor in *An Introduction to the Philosophy of Education,* 1957 describes it as "an excellent book written with a clarity quite exceptional in educational writings." And (ii) the appointment of Louis Arnaud Reid to the first Chair in philosophy of education at the University of London in 1947, a position he held until 1962. Reid had been professor of philosophy at what was to become the University of Newcastle. (He was a visiting professor at the University of British Columbia in 1951.) These events were certainly indications of emerging interest in philosophy of education in Britain and Australia, but the Americans led the way in developing a revitalized philosophy of education in the early 1950s.

15. Christopher J. Lucas (ed.), *What is the Philosophy of Education?* New York: Macmillan, 1969. Reflection on the development of philosophy of education in the twentieth century, already well underway, argues for a reprinting of this invaluable collection.

16. Andrew F. Skinner, "Philosophy of education in Canada: Some impressions and comparative comments," *Canadian Education and Research Digest 3*, 4, 1963: 251-61. Skinner is also the author of *Teachers' Heritage: An Introduction to the Study of Education,* Toronto: Faculty of Education, University of Toronto, 1979, chapter 9 of which offers a general overview of philosophy of education and its relevance to the teacher.

17. See Willard Brehaut, "Educational research in Canada, 1956-8," *Canadian Education 15*, 3, 1960: 37-40. Also his "Educational research in Canada, 1959-61," *Canadian Education and Research Digest 3*, 2, 1963: 128-31.

18. It is perhaps worth noting that developments in Britain were not that far ahead of Canada. Of course, R. S. Peters was on the scene there by 1962 and the explosion of interest in philosophy of education had begun. But just six years earlier, a rarely noted survey of philosophy of education in university teacher education courses in Britain had revealed that only occasionally was there a specific course entitled "Philosophy of education," that the one common element in the various offerings appeared to be the study of Plato, that there was considerable dissatisfaction with the philosophical component in the courses, and that there were only slight indications that the approach might shift from the "great thinkers" model to a philosophical consideration of the nature of education. See M. M. Lewis, "The philosophy of education in courses for graduates," *Universities Quarterly 10*, 3, 1956: 268-72.

(Despite the title of the article, the survey concerned initial teacher education programs.)

19. The conference both reflected developing interest in the subject and helped to further promote it. The proceedings are published as *Philosophy and Education* Monograph Series No. 3, Toronto: Ontario Institute for Studies in Education, 1967. OISE was established in 1965 effectively as the graduate school for educational studies at the University of Toronto. It was decided when OISE was created that philosophers of education would be appointed. In 1967, the Department of Educational Foundations was renamed the Department of History and Philosophy of Education.

20. I can also confirm that, as a doctoral student in philosophy of education at OISE, I had no difficulty in 1969 in finding two helpful and interested faculty members from the department of philosophy in the University of Toronto willing to serve on my supervisory committee.

21. The proceedings are published in C. M. Beck, B. S. Crittenden, and E. V. Sullivan (eds.), *Moral Education: Interdisciplinary Approaches,* Toronto: University of Toronto Press, 1971. The philosophers included Kurt Baier, A. I. Melden, and David Gauthier. Lawrence Kohlberg presented the lead paper.

22. The two public lectures can be found in revised form in R. M. Hare, "Language and moral education," in Glenn Langford and D. J. O'Connor (eds.), *New Essays in Philosophy of Education*, London: Routledge and Kegan Paul, 1973.

23. The proceedings were never published in a general collection, I believe, but most of the papers did appear subsequently in various places. Scheffler's contribution at the conference was his "Philosophy of education and the new activism," reprinted in Scheffler, *Reason and Teaching*, Indianapolis: Bobbs-Merrill, 1973. This is a convenient place to point out that the remark, by Dennis Hewish, about coming from the trenches of teaching to the Pentagon of philosophy only to find the generals playing chess, was made at this conference not at the 1966 conference. Kevin Harris gets this wrong in his *Education and Knowledge*, London: Routledge and Kegan Paul, 1979: 197, fn 29.

24. In the second half of the 1960s, perhaps the two best known examples are: *Living and Learning: The Report of the Provincial Committee on Aims and Objectives of Education in the Schools of Ontario (The Hall-Dennis report)*, Toronto, 1968. And: *Religious Information and Moral Development: The Report of the Committee on Religious Education in the Public Schools of Ontario (The Mackay report)*, Toronto, 1969. These two reports were squarely in the areas of child-centred education and moral education in which philosophers of education were deeply interested, debates which were equally active in Britain and the United States.

25. In an interesting recent discussion, prompted by the 50th anniversary of the Philosophy of Education Society (USA), Clive Beck downplays the influence of British (and Australian) philosophy of education on North American developments. See Clive Beck, "North American, British and Australian Philosophy of Education from 1941 to 1991: Links, Trends, Prospects," *Educational Theory 41*, 3: 311-20. In particular, Beck reminds us that Scheffler preceded Peters on the scene, and that analytical philosophy of education in the United States was already well advanced when the British contributions began to emerge. Beck, however, speaks throughout of North America, lumping the United States and Canada together. His plausible thesis as applied to the U.S. is less plausible when applied specifically to Canada. Here, I believe, influences from both the United States and Britain, together with local interests, combined to provide the stimulus needed to create the active discipline we find today. A number of Canadians went to England in the 1960s to study philosophy of education and returned before the end of the decade bringing

elements of the work of R. S. Peters and Paul Hirst especially into the evolving Canadian field. I do not wish to exaggerate this, as will be clear later, but some distinction between Canada and the United States needs to be drawn. Between Canada and Australia, there was on-going contact and cross-fertilization, though the Australians were off the mark earlier with their journal *Educational Philosophy and Theory* (1969), and with their society (The Philosophy of Education Society of Australasia, 1970), and in the person of John Passmore had a philosopher with an international reputation writing about the philosophy of education. And, of course, a number of Australians, including Beck, Crittenden, and Eastwood, were appointed to positions in Canadian universities in the early days of the resurgence of interest.

26. Many other names could be added to this list. Philosophers of education across the country would surely want to add names of local colleagues in departments of philosophy who have taken a particular interest in philosophy of education. In this, of course, the Canadian scene mirrors that elsewhere. One only has to mention such examples as John Passmore in Australia, R. M. Hare and Antony Flew in Britain, William Frankena in the United States, and Olivier Reboul in France.

27. This matters in various ways, such as having books in philosophy of education reviewed in philosophy journals, having classes in philosophy of education cross-listed between education and philosophy, and having colleagues in philosophy departments available to serve on committees supervising education theses.

28. See, for example, Israel Scheffler (ed.), *Philosophy and Education*, Boston: Allyn and Bacon, 1958. And R. S. Peters, *Authority, Responsibility and Education,* London: George Allen and Unwin, 1959. Discussions of the work of Scheffler and Peters, together with that of Dewey and Russell, can be heard on the cassette tape, *Twentieth Century Philosophy of Education*, William Hare (ed.), School of Education, Dalhousie University, 1990.

29. The statement by the committee, which was accepted by the Philosophy of Education Society (USA), was published in *Educational Theory 4*, 1954: 1-3. It is reprinted in Lucas (ed.), *What is the Philosophy of Education?* op. cit. The statement helped to stimulate the debate referred to earlier in the text.

30. Israel Scheffler, *Philosophy and Education*, op. cit.

31. An introduction to this debate can be found in papers by Soltis and Siegel included in William Hare and John Portelli (eds.), *Philosophy of Education: Introductory Readings*, Calgary: Detselig, 1988. For my own comments, see William Hare, "What can philosophy say to teachers?", in William Hare (ed.), *Reason in Teaching and Education*, Halifax: Dalhousie University School of Education, 1989.

32. CPES is a constituent member of the Canadian Association for the Foundations of Education (CAFE), itself a member of CSSE, but has its own executive and constitution. The President is elected at the annual meeting and serves for two years. The facts of Canadian geography make face-to-face interaction with colleagues elsewhere infrequent, and only a few centres are large enough to have a critical mass of scholars in the discipline, hence the significance of the annual conference within the Learned Societies. As mentioned elsewhere, philosophers of education on the west coast also have the Northwest Philosophy of Education Society. Many Canadians continue to be active participants at the annual (American) PES conference - a few, regrettably, even choosing it to the exclusion of the CPES – and to a lesser extent, at the conference of the corresponding British society. The reality of diminishing travel grants – in some places restricted to one conference a year at most – has effectively ruled out these attractive options for many of us.

33. Views akin to this can be found in: Donald B. Cochrane and Martin Schiralli (eds.), *Philosophy of Education: Canadian Perspectives*, Don Mills: Collier Macmillan, 1982: 4. Also: Michael J. B. Jackson, "Three decades," in John Calam (ed.), *The Study of Education: Canada, 1982*, 9th Yearbook CSSE Vancouver, University of British Columbia, 1982: 93-9. And: Brian Hendley, *Dewey, Russell, Whitehead: Philosophers as Educators*, Carbondale: Southern Illinois University Press, 1986: 127, fn. 10.

34. For a recent example, see Cornel M. Hamm, *Philosophical Issues in Education: An Introduction*, New York: Falmer, 1989.

35. The interest continues. See, for example, Rodger Beehler, *Moral Life*, Totowa: Rowman and Littlefield, 1978; Robert E. Carter, *Dimensions of Moral Education*, Toronto: University of Toronto Press, 1984, and the book mentioned in fn. 59 below.

36. Brian Crittenden, *Form and Content in Moral Education*, Toronto: OISE, 1972. Crittenden returned to Australia in 1973, and has recently written "Philosophy of education in Australia," in John P. Keeves (ed.), *Australian Education: Review of Recent Research*, Sydney: Allen and Unwin, 1987: 3-28.

37. See Clive Beck, *Ethics*, Toronto: McGraw-Hill Ryerson, 1972. Also his *Moral Education in the Schools*, Toronto: OISE, 1971. And Ed Sullivan and Clive Beck, "Moral education," in Niall Byrne and Jack Quarter (eds.), *Must Schools Fail?* Toronto: McClelland and Stewart, 1972: 126-41.

38. See Murray Elliott, "The work of AVER in moral and values education," in *Journal of Education, UBC 21*, 1975: 15-20. Also David M. Williams, "AVER in Surrey: An approach to research and development in moral education," in A. C. Kazepides (ed.), *The Teaching of Values in Canadian Education*, 2nd Yearbook, CSSE, Edmonton: University of Alberta, 1976: 62-75.

39. Harold Entwistle, *Education, Work and Leisure*, London: Routledge and Kegan Paul, 1970: 109.

40. Harold Entwistle, *Child-Centred Education*, London: Methuen, 1970: 216. For Peters on Whitehead, see R. S. Peters, "The philosophy of education," in J. W. Tibble (ed.), *The Study of Education*, London: Routledge and Kegan Paul, 1966: 63. Later on, Peters characterized Whitehead's stages as empirical speculation. See R. S. Peters, "Philosophy of education," in Paul H. Hirst (ed.), *Educational Theory and Its Foundation Disciplines*, London: Routledge and Kegan Paul, 1983: 31.

41. See R. S. Peters, "Education as initiation," in R. D. Archambault (ed.), *Philosophical Analysis and Education*, London: Routledge and Kegan Paul, 1965: 88. Peters was subjected to strong criticism at the 1966 conference as a consultation of the book mentioned in fn. 19 above will reveal.

42. See, for example, Laurence Stott, "The blessed state," *Teacher Education 4*, 1971: 36-41, and his "The myth of the born teacher," in Michael J. Parsons (ed.), *Philosophy of Education 1974*, Edwardsville: Philosophy of Education Society, 1974: 281-91. For another example of existentialist interests, see William Knitter, "Sartrean reflections on education for rational character," *Educational Theory 31*, 3-4, 1981: 307-18.

43. R. F. Dearden, "Philosophy of education, 1952-82," *British Journal of Educational Studies 30*, 1, 1982: 57-71. I am not close enough to the British scene to know if Dearden's observation is true, but one wonders at times if a tradition is not recognized as flourishing because it is thought not to count. It must be admitted, too, that given the dominant image of philosophy of education, those working in other

philosophical traditions sometimes do not want to be counted. Both these attitudes serve to frustrate the exchange of ideas and in the end everyone loses.

44. See his most recent book, *The Tact of Teaching*, London, ON: Althouse Press, 1991. Also his paper "The phenomenology of pedagogic observation," *Canadian Journal of Education 4*, 1, 1979: 5-16.

45. A spot check of half a dozen journals for 1990, i.e. *Studies in Philosophy and Education, Journal of Philosophy of Education, Proceedings of the Philosophy of Education Society, Paideusis, Canadian Journal of Education,* and *Journal of Educational Thought*, reveals more than twenty articles by Canadians, with topics such as moral education, critical thinking, science education, literary education, children's rights, and cultural literacy, not counting a seven paper symposium on philosophy of education in teacher education published in *Paideusis.*

46. Don Cochrane (ed.), *So Much for the Mind*, Toronto: Kagan and Woo, 1987.

47. John McPeck, *Critical Thinking and Education*, Oxford: Martin Robertson, 1981. See also John McPeck, *Teaching Critical Thinking*, New York: Routledge, 1990. A number of other Canadians have contributed to the debate on critical thinking, including Robin Barrow, Jerrold Coombs, Aline Giroux, Mark Selman, and Stephen Norris. See also David Hitchcock, *Critical Thinking: A Guide to Evaluating Information*, Toronto: Methuen, 1983, for a text designed to teach critical thinking.

48. Sharon Bailin, *Achieving Extraordinary Ends: An Essay on Creativity*, Dordrecht: Kluwer, 1988.

49. Eamonn Callan, *Autonomy and Schooling*, Montreal: McGill-Queen's University Press, 1988. In a critical but sympathetic review, Dearden welcomes Callan's book for making autonomy its main organizing theme. See *Journal of Philosophy of Education 24*, 1, 1990: 127-31.

50. See William Hare, *Open-mindedness and Education*, Montreal: McGill-Queen's University Press, 1979. And William Hare, *In Defence of Open-mindedness*, Montreal: McGill-Queen's, 1985. Also chapters 3, 4, and 5 in this collection which extend the discussions in my books on open-mindedness.

51. Brian Hendley, *Dewey, Russell, Whitehead: Philosophers as Educators*, op. cit. Other Canadian philosophers have written on these authors, including Eamonn Callan on Dewey, and Howard Woodhouse on Russell and Whitehead. See also my own discussion of Russell in chapter 2.

52. A more balanced assessment can be found in John P. Portelli, "Analytic philosophy of education: Development and misconceptions," *Journal of Educational Thought 21*, 1, 1987: 20-32.

53. Harold Entwistle, *Antonio Gramsci: Conservative Schooling for Radical Politics*, London: Routledge and Kegan Paul, 1979.

54. Henry Giroux writes of Entwistle's book: "Its raison d'être begins not with a problem or issue to be explored but with a messianic fervor, the purpose of which appears to be to impose a positivistic reading on Gramsci . . ." That is drivel, but replace positivistic with counterhegemonic, and we have a fair assessment of Giroux's critique itself. See Henry A. Giroux, *Teachers as Intellectuals*, Granby, Mass.: Bergin and Harvey, 1988: 198.

55. See *Paideusis 3*, 2, 1991. Jay Newman, who contributes to this special issue, has also written *The Mental Philosophy of John Henry Newman*, Waterloo: Wilfred Laurier University Press, 1986.

56. Robin Barrow, *Giving Teaching Back to Teachers*, London, ON: Althouse Press, 1984.

57. Clive Beck, *Better Schools: A Values Perspective*, New York: Falmer, 1990.

58. Alan Pearson, *The Teacher: Theory and Practice in Teacher Education*, New York: Routledge, 1989.

59. Debra Shogan, *Care and Moral Motivation*, Toronto: OISE Press, 1988. See also her paper "Educating moral emotions," *Paideusis 2*, 1, 1988: 15-28.

60. See "Symposium: Should public education be gender-free?", *Educational Theory 35*, 4, 1985: 345-69.

61. See, for example, Mark Selman and Murray Ross, "Epistemology, practical research, and human subjects," in David P. Ericson (ed.), *Philosophy of Education 1990*, Normal, IL: Philosophy of Education Society, 1990: 319-31.

62. John Dewey, "Lessons from the war," in Jo Ann Boydston (ed.), *John Dewey: The Later Works, Vol. 14, 1939-41*, Carbondale: Southern Illinois University Press, 1988: 325-34.

63. For a selection of work by Canadian philosophers of education who mainly entered the field during the 1980s, see Sharon Bailin and John P. Portelli (eds.), *Reason and Values: New Essays in Philosophy of Education*, Calgary: Detselig Enterprises Ltd., 1993.

2

Russell's Contribution to Philosophy of Education

Bertrand Russell's important contribution to philosophy of education has been largely ignored. This is unfortunate since Russell provides a powerful and illuminating account of the aims of education and the nature of teaching. Russell's work is in the tradition of liberalism in education which opposes indoctrination and authoritarian approaches, and emphasizes respect for students.

Introduction

Bertrand Russell occupies an uncertain position in philosophy of education. Assured of a permanent and distinguished place in the history of philosophy, he is commonly thought to barely qualify as a philosopher of education at all. His extensive writings on education, a body of work which begins well before the first World War and continues until the 1960s and which includes two books, several chapters, and numerous journal and magazine articles, are dismissed as of little philosophical interest. Joe Park, for example, states that "considerable care has been taken [by Park] to speak of Russell's ideas as a theory and not a philosophy of education."[1] Leslie Perry remarks that Russell's philosophy "is singularly separated from his writings on education. He did not subject educational questions to close philosophical analysis."[2] If we view Russell's contributions to educational theory as part of his general work on social and political questions, then we may include here John G. Slater's judgment that Russell made no contribution to political philosophy.[3] Probably A. J. Ayer captures the general sentiment best in his assessment that Russell's writings on social and political questions "express the moral outlook of a humane and enlightened man" but they lack depth and theoretical interest.[4]

These explicit judgments are reflected in the general literature on philosophy of education where Russell is all but ignored. A good example is the once widely used book *The Logic of Education* by Paul Hirst and Richard Peters which contains not a single mention of Russell in the more than six pages devoted to suggestions for further reading in philosophy of education and general philosophy.[5] And yet, as we shall see, Russell has important things to say about many of the topics discussed in this book. Other examples are not hard to find. A surprising one is John White's *The Aims of Education Restated*, which manages not a single reference to Russell while bemoaning the dearth of work on this topic.[6] Again, we will see that Russell had a sustained interest in educational aims. This general neglect carries over into the teaching of philosophy of education. Certainly it was possible twenty years ago to study philosophy of education at the graduate level in Britain and Canada without being put on to

Russell, except perhaps for the deprecating suggestion that "there's always Russell." It would surprise me if, with some honorable exceptions, Russell looms large in philosophy of education classes today. One notes in this context, especially with respect to courses for teachers, the now fashionable view that Russell is dated. Mary Anne Raywid, for example, quotes Russell on the problems of propaganda in education and comments: "Admirable, perhaps, but extensively irrelevant to the indoctrination danger as we are now coming to perceive it."[7]

The neglect by philosophers of education can to some extent be explained if not ultimately defended. Contemporary philosophy of education emerged in the mid-1950s and sought rather self-consciously to become a respectable member of the philosophical family. When Peters and Scheffler came to write their pioneering works, inspiration came from the dominant approach to philosophy, the analysis of concepts. Scheffler noted that "the prospects for philosophical inquiry into education, in the spirit of contemporary analysis and with the help of its methods" seemed encouraging.[8] Peters, in a similar vein, claimed that conceptual clarification was an urgent necessity.[9] This, of course, was the very time when Russell was heaping scorn on general philosophy as then practised. It was concerned, you will recall, with the different ways in which silly people can say silly things.[10] It amounted to "philosophy-without-tears" where the central text was Fowler's *Modern English Usage*.[11] And Russell's famous anecdote about his inquiring the shortest way to Winchester was not calculated to win friends in the philosophical community by which he felt neglected.[12]

We must also acknowledge the fact that in his writings on education Russell makes no attempt to limit his contributions to commentary of a philosophical kind. He is quite willing to offer empirical generalizations based on psychology, general observation, and common sense. For example, he tells us that the impartiality of the learner is best secured by exposing him or her to teachers with opposite prejudices.[13] This is a point which has appealed to other philosophers,[14] and it may well be true, but it is evidently not something which can be known through philosophical reflection. Some of his short essays indeed are mainly psychological in character,[15] but typically perhaps we find different disciplines freely drawn on. This diversity immediately put Russell out of step with the trend towards an emphasis on the distinctive nature of philosophy of education exemplified in the 1954 statement of the (American) Committee on the Nature and Function of the Discipline of the Philosophy of Education.[16] Peters also denounced the undifferentiated approach and viewed what he called the "omnibus conception" of the philosopher's task as "a relic of the old conception of the philosopher as a kind of oracle."[17] There is also in Russell a penchant for the general pronouncement, the value judgment presented as an obvious truth, the "high-level directive" to use Peters' expression. We may or may not agree with Russell that the headmaster should have freedom in the choice of textbooks,[18] that the best teachers are not impartial,[19] that the atmosphere of most progressive schools is too pleasant and too easy-going to be an adequate preparation for modern life,[20] or that the examination system leads students to view knowledge from a purely utilitarian point of view;[21] but we may all agree that these observations are not particularly philosophical in character. The question, however, is whether or not these adequately represent Russell's contribution.

It must also be allowed that a would-be defender is not helped by some of Russell's own comments about his work on education. Slater has quoted Russell's comment that he did not write *Principles of Social Reconstruction* in his capacity as a philosopher.[22] Referring to the books, including his two books on education, quoted by Goldstein in his affidavit submitted during the City College of New York controversy in 1940, Russell asserted that "the books and opinions mentioned are no part of my philosophy and cannot be correctly described as philosophy at all."[23] And in *The Philosophy of Bertrand Russell*, Russell suggests that there is little or no connection between his works of philosophy proper and his writings on education although others had claimed to find one.[24] Before these remarks are taken as decisive, however, some mitigating points may be mentioned. Certainly in 1940, Russell had reason to distinguish sharply between his more theoretical writings and those with a practical emphasis, since his teaching at City College would be confined to the former. But applied philosophy has come to be regarded as a legitimate aspect of general philosophy in recent years, and Russell may well have been employing an overly sharp contrast between the technical and theoretical on the one hand, and the popular and practical on the other. We should not, I think, go along with the suggestion that wanting to improve the world and speaking in plain terms excludes philosophy. But the real test, of course, is whether or not any substantial philosophy can be found in his writings on education.

My own view is that Russell's main contribution to philosophy of education is twofold. First, he makes an important contribution to our understanding of that fundamental distinction which we have come to speak of as the distinction between education and indoctrination. And second, he formulates and defends a conception of teaching appropriate to the ideal of education. Let us consider these points in turn.

The Nature of Education

Russell rightly sees that questions about the aims of education are fundamental: "Before considering how to educate, it is well to be clear as to the sort of result which we wish to achieve."[25] But a consideration of aims might degenerate into nothing more than a rhetorical defence of certain outcomes. In the general literature on education, we encounter vague but appealing comments, for example, that education is of the whole person. Disconcertingly, we also run into the view that "any good education must be narrow."[26] These remarks could in themselves only be deemed philosophical in that broad sense which applies to a person's general outlook. What would turn a discussion into something more genuinely philosophical would be an attempt to explain what a certain aim involves, to provide an interpretation and characterization, or to show why a certain aim matters. Ironically, Joe Park complains that Russell "has failed to formulate a comprehensive, yet direct, simple and concise statement of the aims of education."[27] This complaint totally misses the point that what Russell has done is to critically examine the aims of education.

Contemporary philosophers of education have shown that the concept of education implies certain criteria to which learning and teaching in schools should but do not always conform. This thesis has been supported by appeal to analogy, examples, what we would say in certain cases and so on. Russell does not argue for this point in any detail but it is clear that he recognizes it. He tells us, for example, that the modern teacher is appointed by an education authority but dismissed if found to be educating.[28] On another occasion, Russell says that he is conscious of being rash but nevertheless doubts whether an education designed to prevent thought is the best possible.[29] In his own way, he is making the point that often what passes for education, what is called education, falls short of any serious conception of education. Moreover, implicit in these barbs is a concern for truth and a conception of education as intimately connected with free inquiry which runs throughout Russell's work. I think it is fair to say that a large part of Russell's concern with the aims of education is to show how education differs from indoctrination and how conceptual clarity can help prevent confusion here. We are always in danger of failing to recognize the differences.

Russell's chief technique is to point out certain distinctions, often simple but overlooked, which serve to forestall tempting lines of thought and to illuminate the concept in question. For example, it is often assumed that indoctrination is either inevitable in teaching because children do not have the ability to exercise genuine freedom of choice at an early age, or justifiable because we would not let them make independent decisions until they are more mature. (Russell wants to know if children are to be free to swallow pins.)[30] His solution is to distinguish between giving freedom to the child and giving the child a preparation for freedom.[31] Without this distinction,[32] we are likely to become cavalier about the difference between education and indoctrination and easy prey for those who want to promote indoctrination.

It will be argued, for example, that respect for existing institutions is surely important, and the intuitively desirable overtones of "respect" may pave the way for political indoctrination. Here Russell reminds us of the differences between blind respect and thinking respect which is based on a recognition of merit.[33] That is, some forms of respect have to be earned, and we need to exercise our critical faculties to determine if respect is *deserved.* Unfortunately, as Russell sees it, state education typically attempts to instil admiration for existing institutions while repressing critical appraisal.[34] As we shall see subsequently, Russell is also aware of respect for persons, a respect we owe to others which does not have to be earned. The general point to be noticed here is that Russell shows how conceptual carelessness can fuel misguided theories and miseducative practices.

Russell anticipates the objection that free thought may lead people to choose or believe what is wrong rather than right.[35] In this, of course, Russell is not merely toying with imaginary opponents. It is not difficult to find those who assert that an emphasis on the individual's critical faculties, free expression and general discussion, leads to a situation where "every truth is treated as a potential untruth, and every untruth as a potential truth. Thus the very concept of truth recedes into a nebulous background: a goal never to be attained."[36] And it is clear in practice that those who indoctrinate are encouraged by their own powerful conviction that their ideas are true and in danger of being ignored. Alberta's Jim Keegstra is a case in point, as we shall see later in chapter six. Where, it will be asked, is our own professed concern and respect for truth if we tolerate open criticism? Russell, I believe, has shown us the way through this philosophical tangle.

First, he distinguishes between the wish for truth and the conviction that some particular creed is the truth.[37] Russell sometimes captures this as the distinction between truth and truthfulness, and he characterizes the latter as "the habit of forming our opinions on the evidence, and holding them with that degree of conviction which the evidence warrants."[38] He adds that we must always be ready to admit new evidence against previous beliefs. Russell develops this distinction in several places in his writings. At times it appears as the principle of *veracity* which "consists in trying to be right in matters of belief, and also in doing what is possible to insure that others are right."[39] Respect for truth then requires that we be prepared to reconsider what we have until now taken as true.

Second, Russell shows that a concern for truthfulness or veracity does not entail scepticism where the very notion of truth vanishes. He rejects the either-or dilemma represented by a choice between scepticism and dogmatism, and defends what he himself describes as a kind of half-way house[40] where truth is ascertainable with difficulty to a certain degree. The rational person "accepts the most probable hypothesis for the time being while continuing to look for new evidence to confirm or confute it."[41] Russell would not concede that there is a contradiction between having a profound respect for truth and seeing what we take to be true as potentially untrue, as Niemeyer argues, because if our respect is indeed a thinking respect, it will accept and welcome new evidence which overturns an earlier belief. Respect for truth is incompatible with the dogmatic conviction that some particular belief is true.

Third, and following from this, Russell draws the important distinction between the opinions a person has and the way in which they are held.[42] This latter aspect refers to an attitude or outlook which is central to Russell's conception of education. If we assess a person as educated or not on the basis of whether or not his or her beliefs are actually true, we encounter the problem that the available evidence may have led this person to the wrong conclusion. An example of this concerning Russell himself is the fact that, like many others, he accepted the Piltdown skull as genuine.[43] What is crucial, however, is how the person reacts in the light of emerging evidence. It was this attitude which Russell attempted to describe throughout his writings on education: from an early essay on education in 1913 when he spoke of the scientific attitude of mind as involving an attempt to view the evidence frankly, without preconceptions and without bias;[44] to his final thoughts on education almost half a century later when he characterized the undogmatic temper as involving continual search and avoidance of comfortable certainty.[45]

No doubt, as Stephen Jay Gould has put it, we are all locked into the "search images" of our specializations.[46] We notice what we are interested in, and I could not help but notice that Russell has a good deal to say about open-mindedness and its place in education. The points just mentioned obviously have a close bearing on this concept. But Russell makes the connection between education and open-mindedness explicit. It is generally well known, I think, that Russell declared that open-mindedness should be one of the qualities that education aims at producing.[47] No doubt, out of context, this must sound like the kind of grandiloquent pronouncement scorned by R. S. Peters in his reference to the image of the philosopher as oracle. But it would be a mistake to dismiss Russell in this way, for we would fail to see how he has helped to clarify this attitude.

First, Russell sees clearly that open-mindedness is not incompatible with having convictions and, therefore, does not presuppose neutrality. We noted earlier that he speaks of holding beliefs with that degree of conviction which the evidence warrants. He points out that "the difference between a rational man and a dogmatist is not that the latter has beliefs while the former has none. The difference is as to the grounds of the beliefs and the way in which they are held."[48] The point would have been even clearer if Russell had more carefully distinguished between having an open mind in the sense of having as yet formed no view, and being open-minded in the sense of having a certain attitude, both of which are discussed and somewhat run together in his interesting paper "Can We Afford to Have Open Minds?"[49] Certainly, Russell is right to say that if you preserve an open mind all the time and about everything, you will accomplish nothing, but this should not be construed as a reflection on open-mindedness as an attitude. Russell himself sees this because elsewhere he makes the point that the rational person "will be prepared to act upon a high degree of probability as vigorously as the dogmatist acts upon what he holds to be certainty."[50] But this point is not clear to everyone, as I have shown elsewhere,[51] and part of the confusion is thinking of having an open mind and being open-minded as synonymous. This last quotation shows, I believe, that when, in a paper written in 1964,[52] Russell calls on philosophers to take immediate action in so far as they can help end the arms race, he is not departing from an earlier view. He had *consistently* championed vigorous action on a high degree of probability.

Second, Russell helps us to see that open-mindedness means neither scepticism nor credulity. As for the latter, open-mindedness does not involve being willing to believe whatever you are told but being willing to consider the possibility that something is true. As Russell puts it, "education in credulity leads by quick stages to mental decay."[53] And elsewhere, he writes, "Instead of credulity, the object should be to stimulate constructive doubt."[54] This remark brings us face to face with the question of scepticism. Now certainly Russell does introduce the notion of doubt here as he does elsewhere to illuminate the concept of open-mindedness. And in my first book, I chided him with making the link, though I did concede that the particular comment cited occurred in a piece of correspondence, and might be interpreted as pragmatic advice.[55] Nevertheless, on reflection it seems a trifle ungenerous, given that Russell makes considerable effort to dissociate his position from that of scepticism. He sees it as equally important for education to counteract incredulity as credulity.[56] It is relevant too that Russell speaks of *constructive* doubt, doubt which has a basis, and which is designed to lead to a better appreciation of the truth. Russell wants students to learn to be immune to eloquence but not to become immune to argument and evidence.[57] Indeed, his view is that "towards facts, submission is the only rational attitude."[58] Thus, his scepticism is a tempered and limited one, and his position on open-mindedness is a good example of what Herbert Feigl characterized as the policy which "steers a sane middle course between the extremes of dogmatism and skepticism."[59]

Third, Russell recognizes that there comes a time when open-mindedness is virtually without merit from a practical point of view, though some of his illustrations, for example the disappearance of open-mindedness with respect to whom you might marry once you have chosen a wife, ring a little odd coming from him. But the point is clear enough. Certain decisions tend to close doors, and we cannot always reconsider them. Career decisions are one example. Even here, however, as Russell points out, there is a certain residual open-mindedness which is important, since circumstances might arise in which your decision would need to be reexamined. Russell's example is of a lawyer in a country that becomes totalitarian.[60]

Finally, Russell shows more clearly than any other writer I have encountered what the false face of open-mindedness looks like. It appears as what he calls "good form":

> "Good form" is quite compatible with a superficial open-mindedness, a readiness to hear all sides, and a certain urbanity towards opponents. But it is not compatible with fundamental open-mindedness, or with any inward readiness to give weight to the other side. Its essence is the assumption that what is important is a certain kind of behaviour, a behaviour which minimizes friction between

equals and delicately impresses inferiors with a conviction of their own crudity.[61]

What is important here is the point that open-mindedness really requires a certain attitude, and behavior can superficially mimic this. The ascription of open-mindedness calls for judgment and cannot be mechanically read off from a check list of behaviors. I think that implicit also is a distinction between open-mindedness and tolerance, since those with "good form" do at least tolerate their opponents. This distinction is important, I believe, since tolerance does not make the same demands on an individual as open- mindedness. I may tolerate your views but never be willing to ask seriously if they undermine my own. Hence, when Russell claims elsewhere that one source of tolerance is the realization that we may be mistaken,[62] this should not be interpreted as the claim that the tolerant individual is *necessarily* impressed with his or her own fallibility.

A proper grasp of these points is still extremely relevant to the indoctrination debate. We shall see later in the Keegstra case, for example, how the fundamental link between open-mindedness and respect for evidence, which Russell insisted on, can be lost sight of. We may wonder, then, why Russell's contribution here has been dismissed as largely irrelevant. The charge comes from Mary Anne Raywid who takes exception to one of Russell's practical suggestions to teachers who wish to combat indoctrination, namely that they expose their students to the most vehement and terrific argumentation on all sides of every question. This prompts Raywid to remark, as I noted earlier, that this is admirable but irrelevant, just the kind of deprecating and dismissive comment which is all too common.[63]

The nub of her objection is that indoctrination can occur as an osmosis-like process which infiltrates the very language we learn and indeed the whole process of upbringing. In response, two points need to be made at once. First, despite Raywid's claim that she has personally identified this new form of indoctrination, it seems abundantly clear that Russell was quite familiar with it. Russell speaks of the person who "goes through life imprisoned in the prejudices derived from common sense, from the habitual beliefs of his age or his nation, and from convictions which have grown up in his mind without the co-operation or consent of his deliberate reason."[64] His reference elsewhere to the paradox of "using language to undo the false beliefs that it suggests,"[65] shows that Russell was not unaware of what Raywid calls a ubiquitous and pervasive form of indoctrination. The suggestion of naivete is wide of the mark. Second, it is not at all clear that Russell's positive suggestion is as pointless as Raywid implies. In examining particular controversies in the manner advocated by Russell, there is no reason to assume that what one learns is confined to the details of the particular issue at hand. Students may in addition be developing habits of questioning which will lead them to be more critical of beliefs which tend to be taken for granted.

It would be a pity if this single reference to a practical suggestion were to create the impression that Russell has no philosophical contribution to make to our understanding of indoctrination. It would be similarly mistaken to assume that with respect to teaching itself all Russell has to offer is practical advice. We need to recognize that any such advice he has to offer is shaped by a general view of what teaching ought to be.

A Conception of Teaching

If Russell's contribution were limited to such practical aspects of teaching as his suggestion for dealing with controversial material by exposing students to "the most eloquent advocates of every imaginable point of view,"[66] the neglect of his work by philosophers of education might be justified. Interesting as these remarks are, they are no substitute for a clear and defensible account of teaching itself. I believe that we do find an important conception of teaching detailed in Russell's work, one which foreshadows an influential strand in contemporary philosophy of education. Russell's contribution here has not been adequately acknowledged. Moreover, it is a conception which blends perfectly with his account of education distinguished from indoctrination.

We can appreciate this if we pause to consider some further remarks of a rather practical nature about teaching controversial materials which might at first glance seem questionable given his commitment to open-mindedness as an aim of education. There is, for example, Russell's view that all teachers, not only those at the university level,[67] must be free to express their opinions even if these differ from the prevailing orthodoxy. Along with some recent writers,[68] we may wonder if such a departure from neutrality is conducive to the development of open-mindedness in the students. Moreover, Russell qualifies the claim by insisting that no fault must be found with the actual knowledge of the students.[69] Is this consistent with his professed belief in the fallibility of knowledge claims which justifies the call for open-mindedness? And finally, we might wonder at his suggestion that one function of the teacher is to mitigate the heat of current controversy.[70] How is this to be reconciled with the view that students must be exposed to the most vehement and terrific argumentation on all sides of every question in order to offset fanaticism?

The answer to these puzzles is simply that behind Russell's particular suggestions for practice lies a view about the *attitude* which any teacher needs to bring to the task. And this attitude can be captured in two notions: reverence and humility. Russell's primary concern is not with the methods of teaching at all but with the attitude of the teacher whatever method is used. Even in those general essays where Russell deals with topics such as play, drill, and class size, it is significant that he closes with the point that teachers need a more liberal *outlook*.[71] It is true that Russell is on record as having made a vow as an undergraduate that when he became a university teacher he would place no faith in the lecture method.[72] But elsewhere he makes it clear that instruction can be given in a liberal *spirit* though this does not always occur.[73] He describes his own undergraduate experiences at Cambridge in the 1890s as a process of indoctrination.[74] In considering Russell, we should not be misled by the label "progressive" to think primarily of methods.

"Reverence" is a somewhat old-fashioned term for a modern idea, namely that the teacher must respect the students as individuals. The child is not a piece of clay to be moulded into shape, but is capable of developing into an adult who can exercise independent and reasonable judgment. Teachers whose objective it is to have students adopt their opinions rather than to come to think for themselves lack reverence. The student must be regarded as an end in himself or herself,[75] not as raw material to be used for some other purpose. If education is to produce thought rather than belief, another distinction drawn by Russell,[76] then teachers need a spirit of reverence. Incidentally, Russell is not suggesting that students do not need to respect their teachers: "You do have to have enough respect for the teacher to enable the business of teaching to be carried on."[77] The danger is that respect for the teacher will turn into unthinking respect, which undermines independent thought. An element of authority is necessary, but for Russell it is very much a provisional authority. Freedom of opinion, which Russell regards as the most important kind of freedom, belongs also to the pupil,[78] and respect entails fostering free inquiry on the part of the student. Too often it is checked by dogma or stony silence.[79]

In part, Russell is setting out a straightforward moral demand when he speaks of reverence. There is also a moral aspect to humility, for Russell refers to the responsibility which falls on the teacher because of the position of trust he or she is in.[80] In addition, however, there is an epistemological basis for these requirements. Teachers need to respect the opinions of their students because teachers may learn that their own views are mistaken, unclear, or susceptible of improvement. Respect for students requires a liberal outlook in teaching which Russell defines as one which "regards all questions as open to discussion and all opinions as open to a greater or less measure of doubt."[81] Humility is appropriate given the probability that the opinions we express as teachers will turn out to be erroneous:

> ... if you state an opinion, you should realize that, if you take opinions held by people three hundred years ago, you will find very few that you would think right now, and in the same way there must be few of our opinions now that are right.[82]

Here, I think, we do not need to look far for a link with Russell's general philosophical view. For example, Russell holds that the greater part of what would commonly pass as knowledge is more or less probable opinion.[83] Again, he interprets perfect rationality not as believing what is true but as attaching to every proposition a degree of belief corresponding to its degree of credibility.[84] These general epistemological ideas explain and justify the emphasis on humility. Russell dispenses with the notion of the teacher as the authoritative source of knowledge, and substitutes a view which sees the teacher as a co-inquirer, more familiar than the students with the field, but aware of his or her limitations.

In expressing his or her views on a controversial topic, a teacher with a liberal outlook is not trying to secure passive acceptance. The Keegstra case may make us incline towards teacher neutrality, but Keegstra lacked respect for his students, and humility. These function as guidelines for the teacher who wants to foster the student's independent judgment, and Russell acknowledges that teachers will simply have to *find* a way of acting in accordance with the spirit of liberty.[85] There are no hard and fast methodological rules.

In requiring that the examination of controversy not be at the expense of knowledge, Russell can be interpreted as meaning that teachers must acquaint their students with those views which are widely *regarded* as constituting knowledge. There is no excuse for ignorance and incompetence. We have already met Russell's view that submission is the only rational attitude towards facts, and that is one kind of humility. At the same time, however, we need that humility which leaves us prepared to review what we have thus far counted as knowledge.[86] Russell also recognizes that an accusation of incompetence can be used to silence unpopular opinions, hence he proposed that "teachers should be chosen for their expertness in the subject they teach, and the judges of this expertness should be other experts."[87]

When Russell suggests that one function of the teacher is to mitigate the heat of current controversy, his idea is not to play down or ignore the fact of controversy but rather to stress the importance of helping students become "rather impervious to eloquence and propaganda."[88] Students need *exposure* to propaganda, but they need to develop the critical skills which will prevent them from being taken in by it. They need to form their views on the available evidence and hold them no more firmly than the evidence warrants. Respect here means refraining from engaging in propaganda oneself in teaching, and humility involves recognizing that one is not in a position to resolve the controversy. What one can and should do as a teacher is to promote the development of impartial and disinterested judgment.[89]

It is important to recognize that, in calling for reverence, Russell is not indulging in any kind of romantic tender-mindedness.[90] Students are to be encouraged to form their own opinions, but these must be based on a careful review of the evidence and an appraisal of the relevant arguments. The teachers should "try to teach impartiality of judgment, the habit of searching for impersonal truth, and distrust of party catchwords."[91] Russell is not defending a relativistic approach where opinions are deemed equal. Towards the opinions of others, the objective is to produce "only such opposition as is combined with imaginative apprehension and a clear realization of the grounds of opposition."[92] In recognizing the importance of creative work by students, Russell warns against encouraging students to think that they are producing great works of art. Teachers, he says, "must learn to respect intelligence and independent thought where it exists, though they need not, like some progressive educators, pretend to find it in all and sundry."[93] Respect for the student requires a critical stance in teaching.

Some commentators have questioned Russell's own commitment to these fundamental attributes of teaching. Brian Hendley admits to having "the uncomfortable feeling that Russell wants to replace bigotry and narrow-mindedness with an intolerance of his very own."[94] He quotes Katherine Tait's observation that at Beacon Hill School there was never a cogent presentation of the Christian faith by a believer.[95] More ominously, perhaps, she reports that making up one's mind usually meant agreeing with Russell who invariably knew more than any of the pupils. Here, however, we do need to keep in mind the distinction between theory and practice. Certainly at the level of principle, there is no reason to think that Russell supports a double standard. The clearest evidence of his commitment to an even-handed policy is Russell's own condemnation of state education in France which he regards as militantly secular and as dogmatic as the church schools.[96] This comment makes it unlikely, I think, that Russell's *attitude* can be captured, as Hendley claims, in the remark made on another occasion that he was not prepared to tell children anything he did not believe.[97] This is altogether too cavalier.

Russell's emphasis on respect for the student and the importance of reason in teaching places him in the vanguard of a movement which in our own day is best exemplified in the work of Israel Scheffler and, more recently, Harvey Siegel. Scheffler, in a well known passage, characterized teaching as "an activity aimed at the achievement of learning, and practised in such manner as to respect the student's intellectual integrity and capacity for independent judgment."[98] He viewed this characterization as setting teaching apart from other activities such as propaganda which seek to modify the person without genuinely engaging his or her judgment. Scheffler saw teaching as requiring us to reveal our reasons to the students and to submit them to his or her evaluation and criticism.

Currently, the leading exponent of this conception of teaching is Harvey Siegel who acknowledges his indebtedness to Scheffler.[99] Siegel speaks of the *critical manner* of teaching which he analyzes in terms of the student's right to question and demand reasons, and the teacher's willingness to subject all beliefs and practices to critical scrutiny. It is clear that the critical *manner* refers to certain criteria or standards which teaching should meet *whatever form it takes*.[100] One implication of the term "manner" in this context is that the conception is not being identified with a particular methodology.

Throughout Russell's writings on education, with his consistent theme of evidence, honesty, and a liberal outlook in teaching, we find the forerunner of the critical manner conception. The parallel is striking, yet equally striking is the absence, until recently, of Russell's name in any list of acknowledgements.

Concluding Comment

Joe Park has suggested that "Russell's ideas on education should be treated as hypotheses, formulated by a widely read and very wise man, which remain to be substantiated by scientific investigation."[101] This remark may apply to many of Russell's educational ideas, but it completely ignores all of those ideas, such as we have examined here, which are not advanced as scientific hypotheses at all but as conceptual commentary on certain educational ideals. Russell's task is the traditional philosophical one of clarification and justification. His achievement is to have improved our understanding of education and teaching as ideals, with an analysis which is still relevant. All of the crucial points which we need to sort our way through the Keegstra tangle, for example, are to be found in Russell, set out with inimitable clarity. When the dust settles on the skirmishing in recent philosophy of education, Russell will be seen as an important contributor to the development of the discipline and not as a dinosaur out of place in a new world.[102]

Notes

1. Joe Park, *Bertrand Russell On Education,* London: George Allen and Unwin, 1964: 16

2. Leslie R. Perry (Ed.), *Bertrand Russell, A. S. Neill, Homer Lane, W. H. Kilpatrick: Four Progressive Educators,* London: Collier-Macmillan, 1967: 20.

3. John G. Slater, "The political philosophy of Bertrand Russell," in J. E. Thomas and Kenneth Blackwell (eds.), *Russell in Review,* Toronto: Samuel Stevens, Hakkert, 1976: 135-154.

4. A. J. Ayer, "Bertrand Russell as a philosopher," in Thomas and Blackwell (eds.), *Russell in Review,* op. cit.: 177-202. See also, A. J. Ayer, "An appraisal of Bertrand Russell's philosophy," in D. F. Pears (ed.), *Bertrand Russell: A Collection of Critical Essays,* New York: Anchor Books, 1972 : 6-22.

5. P. H. Hirst and R. S. Peters, *The Logic of Education,* London: Routledge and Kegan Paul, 1970.

6. John White, *The Aims of Education Restated,* London: Routledge and Kegan Paul 1982.

7. Mary Anne Raywid, "Perspectives on the struggle against indoctrination," *Educational Forum 48,* 2, 1984: 137-54.

8. Israel Scheffler, *The Language of Education,* Springfield: Charles C. Thomas, 1960: 8.

9. R. S. Peters, "Education as initiation," in R. D. Archambault (ed.), *Philosophical Analysis and Education,* London: Routledge and Kegan Paul, 1965: 88.

10. Bertrand Russell, *My Philosophical Development,* London: George Allen and Unwin, 1959: 230.

11. Russell, op. cit.: 231

12. Bertrand Russell, *Bertrand Russell Speaks His Mind,* New York: World Publishing Company, 1960: 16.

13. Bertrand Russell and Dora Russell, *Prospects of Industrial Civilization,* New York: Century Co., 1923: 255.

14. Kai Neilsen, "The very idea of a religious education," *Journal of Education (Nova Scotia)* 2, 2, 1974-5: 36-8.

15. For example, "Modern tendencies in education," *The Spectator*, 13 June, 1931: 926-7. And "Free speech in childhood," *The New Statesman and Nation*, 30 May, 1931: 486-8.

16. Commissioned by the Philosophy of Education Society, the text is reprinted in Christopher J. Lucas (ed.), *What is Philosophy of Education?* London: Collier-Macmillan, 1969: 111-3.

17. R. S. Peters, "The philosophy of education," in J. W. Tibble (ed.), *The Study of Education*, London: Routledge and Kegan Paul, 1966: 64.

18. Bertrand Russell and Dora Russell, *Prospects of Industrial Civilization*, op. cit.: 255.

19. op. cit.: 255

20. Bertrand Russell, "As school opens - The educators examined," *The New York Times Magazine*, 7 September, 1952: 9, 44-4.

21. Bertrand Russell, *Principles of Social Reconstruction*, London: George Allen and Unwin, 1916: 162.

22. John G. Slater, "The political philosophy of Bertrand Russell," op. cit.: 138.

23. See Barry Feinberg and Ronald Kasrils, *Bertrand Russell's America*, Volume One 1896-1945, London: George Allen and Unwin, 1973: 159

24. P. A. Schilpp (ed.), *The Philosophy of Bertrand Russell*, New York: Tudor Publishing, 1951: 727.

25. Bertrand Russell, *On Education*, London: Unwin Books, 1971: 28. (Originally published 1926.)

26. Richard Livingstone, *Some Tasks for Education*, Toronto: Oxford University Press, 1946: 17.

27. Joe Park, *Bertrand Russell on Education*, op. cit.: 130.

28. Bertrand Russell, "Freedom versus authority in education," in his *Sceptical Essays* London: George Allen and Unwin, 1928: 187.

29. Bertrand Russell and Dora Russell, *Prospects of Industrial Civilization*, op. cit.: 250.

30. Russell, "Freedom versus authority in education," op. cit.: 184.

31. Bertrand Russell, *John Stuart Mill* (pamphlet), London: Oxford University Press, 1955: 57.

32. See, for example, Harvey Siegel, "Critical thinking as an intellectual right," in D. Moshman (ed.), *Children's Intellectual Rights,* San Francisco: Jossey Bass, 1986: 39-45.

33. Bertrand Russell, "Education for democracy," *Addresses and Proceedings of the National Education Association 77*, (2-6 July) 1939: 532.

34. Bertrand Russell, "Freedom versus authority in education," op. cit.: 186.

35. Bertrand Russell, *John Stuart Mill*, op. cit.: 57.

36. Gerhart Niemeyer, "A reappraisal of the doctrine of free speech," *Thought 25*, 97, 1950: 251-74.

37. Bertrand Russell, *Principles of Social Reconstruction,* op. cit.: 154.

38. Bertrand Russell, "Freedom versus authority in education," op. cit.: 197.

39. Bertrand Russell, "The value of free thought," in his *Understanding History*, New York: Philosophical Library, 1957: 73.

40. Bertrand Russell, "Education for democracy," op. cit.: 529.

41. Bertrand Russell, "Why fanaticism brings defeat," *The Listener*, 23 September, 1948: 452-3.

42. Bertrand Russell, "The value of free thought," op. cit.: 57-8.

43. Bertrand Russell, *Understanding History*, op. cit.: 11.

44. Bertrand Russell, "The place of science in liberal education," in his *Mysticism and Logic*, Harmondsworth: Penguin Books, 1954: 38-49. Elsewhere, I have described this as Russell's first published essay on education, but perhaps we should recognize his paper "The study of mathematics," written in 1902 and published in 1907, now available in Richard A. Rempel et al. (eds.), *The Collected Papers of Bertrand Russell Vol. 12*, London: George Allen and Unwin, 1985: 85-93.

45. Bertrand Russell, "University education," in his *Fact and Fiction*, London: George Allen and Unwin, 1961: 150-56.

46. Stephen Jay Gould, "We first stood on our own two feet in Africa," *Discover*, May 1986: 52-6.

47. Bertrand Russell, *On Education*, op. cit.: 43.

48. Bertrand Russell, "Why fanaticism brings defeat," op. cit.: 452.

49. Bertrand Russell, "Can we afford open minds?" *The New York Times Magazine*, 11 June 1950: 9, 37-8.

50. Bertrand Russell, "Why fanaticism brings defeat," op. cit.: 452.

51. William Hare, *In Defence of Open-mindedness*, Montreal: McGill-Queen's University Press, 1985.

52. Bertrand Russell, "The duty of a philosopher in this age," in Eugene Freeman, (ed.), *The Abdication of Philosophy*, La Salle, Ill.: Open Court, 1976: 15-22.

53. Bertrand Russell, *Principles of Social Reconstruction*, op. cit.: 155.

54. op. cit.: 156.

55. William Hare, *Open-mindedness and Education*, Montreal: McGill-Queen's University Press, 1979.

56. Bertrand Russell, "Education for democracy," op. cit.: 530.

57. op. cit.: 530.

58. Bertrand Russell, "The value of free thought," op. cit.: 102.

59. Herbert Feigl, "The outlook of scientific humanism," in Freeman (ed.), *The Abdication of Philosophy*, op. cit.: 74.

60. Bertrand Russell, "Can we afford open minds?" op. cit.: 9.

61. Bertrand Russell, *Principles of Social Reconstruction*, op. cit.: 152-3.

62. Bertrand Russell, "Why fanaticism brings defeat," op. cit.: 452.

63. See earlier fn. 7. The comment by Russell occurs in "Education for democracy," op. cit.: 529.

64. Bertrand Russell, *The Problems of Philosophy,* London: Oxford University Press, 1973 (1912): 91.

65. Bertrand Russell, *Human Knowledge: Its Scope and Limits,* London: George Allen and Unwin, 1948: 76.

66. Bertrand Russell, "Education for democracy," op. cit.: 529.

67. Bertrand Russell and Dora Russell, *Prospects of Industrial Civilization,* op. cit.: 252.

68. For example, John Wilson, "Education and the neutrality of the teacher," *Journal of Christian Education 14*, 3, 1971: 178.

69. Bertrand Russell and Dora Russell, *Prospects of Industrial Civilization,* op. cit.: 252.

70. Bertrand Russell, "The functions of a teacher," *Unpopular Essays,* London: George Allen and Unwin, 1950: 152.

71. See Bertrand Russell, "As school opens - The educators examined," op. cit.: 45. See also chapter 8 in the present collection for further discussion of Russell's views on attitudes in teaching.

72. Bertrand Russell, "University education," in Russell's *Fact and Fiction,* op. cit.: 154.

73. Bertrand Russell, *Principles of Social Reconstruction,* op. cit.: 149.

74. Bertrand Russell, *My Philosophical Development,* London: George Allen and Unwin, 1959: 11.

75. Bertrand Russell, "Freedom and authority in education," op. cit.: 201.

76. Bertrand Russell, *Principles of Social Reconstruction,* op. cit.: 153.

77. Bertrand Russell, "Education for democracy," op. cit.: 532.

78. Bertrand Russell, "Freedom versus authority in education," op. cit.: 196.

79. Bertrand Russell, *Principles of Social Reconstruction,* op. cit.: 152.

80. op. cit.: 147.

81. Bertrand Russell, "Freedom and the colleges," in Feinberg and Kasrils, *Bertrand Russell's America,* op. cit.: 299-307.

82. Bertrand Russell, "Education for democracy," op. cit.: 533.

83. Bertrand Russell, *The Problems of Philosophy,* op. cit.: 81.

84. Bertrand Russell, *Human Knowledge,* op. cit.: 415.

85. Bertrand Russell, *Principles of Social Reconstruction,* op. cit.: 146.

86. Bertrand Russell, "University education," op. cit.: 156.

87. Bertrand Russell, "Freedom and the colleges," op. cit.: 299.

88. Bertrand Russell, "Education for democracy," op. cit.: 530.

89. Russell typically condemns propaganda where we might more naturally speak of indoctrination.

90. My view on this is disputed by Howard Woodhouse in his paper "More than mere musings: Russell's reflections on education as philosophy," *Russell 7*, 2, 1987-8: 176-8.

91. Bertrand Russell and Dora Russell, *Prospects of Industrial Civilization,* op. cit.: 270.

92. Bertrand Russell, *Principles of Social Reconstruction,* op. cit.: 155-6.

93. Bertrand Russell, "As school opens - The educators examined," op. cit.: 45.

94. Brian Hendley, *Dewey, Russell, Whitehead: Philosophers as Educators,* op. cit.: 71.

95. Katherine Tait, *My Father Bertrand Russell,* New York: Harcourt, Brace, Jovanovich, 1975: 94.

96. Bertrand Russell, *Principles of Social Reconstruction,* op. cit.: 152.

97. Brian Hendley, *Dewey, Russell, Whitehead: Philosophers as Educators,* op. cit.: 72.

98. Israel Scheffler, "Philosophical models of teaching," in R. S. Peters (ed.), *The Concept of Education,* London: Routledge and Kegan Paul, 1967: 120-34.

99. Harvey Siegel, "Critical thinking as an intellectual right," op. cit.: 41. More recently, Siegel has acknowledged Russell's place in this tradition. See Harvey Siegel, "The role of reasons in (science) education," in William Hare (ed.), *Reason in Teaching and Education,* Halifax: Dalhousie University, 1989: 5-21.

100. See the work of John Passmore who has also emphasized the critical spirit in teaching. He seems to identify the critical spirit with particular methods, notably the discussion method. On the other hand, one might interpret his remarks not as practical, methodological advice but as suggestions about further criteria. That is, teaching, whatever form it takes, must manifest the spirit of discussion. See his "On teaching to be critical," in Peters (ed.), *The Concept of Education,* op. cit.: 192-211; also "Education and adaptation for the future," in Donald J. Ortner (ed.), *How Humans Adapt,* Washington: Smithsonian, 1983: 457-76; and especially *The Philosophy of Teaching,* London: Duckworth, 1980, chapter 9.

101. Joe Park, *Bertrand Russell On Education,* op. cit.: 129.

102. A further discussion of Russell as a philosopher of education can be heard in my talk on Russell on the cassette *Twentieth Century Philosophy of Education,* William Hare (ed.), available from School of Education, Dalhousie University, Halifax, NS.

3
Open-mindedness in the Classroom

A number of misunderstandings about open-mindedness persist with the result that inappropriate and misleading practical suggestions are offered to teachers. The use of certain words by the teacher is taken to indicate the absence of this attitude; certain teaching methods and procedures are deemed essential and others incompatible; and some subjects are thought to have a special relationship to open-mindedness. These and other claims are reviewed, and it becomes clear that the trouble arises primarily from philosophical confusion.

Introduction

There is wide-spread agreement that open-mindedness is a disposition to form and revise one's views in the light of evidence and argument, and that this disposition is an important one for education to cultivate. Universal agreement, of course, is not to be found. Despite Dewey's very clear admonition,[1] open-mindedness is still occasionally misinterpreted as empty-mindedness, a mistake which provokes sharp reminders.[2] There is, in addition, considerable disagreement about how open-mindedness relates to other ideas like doubt, confidence, commitment, and neutrality, and confused thinking here generates some hesitation about open-mindedness as an aim of education.[3] Other writers, perhaps believing that intellectual aspects of education have been over-emphasized, make little mention of open-mindedness in their discussion of educational aims.[4]

Open-mindedness does not imply relativism if that position is understood to involve the claim that there is no way of rationally deciding between conflicting claims. Indeed, if this view is taken seriously, open-mindedness must vanish as an ideal. The drift towards relativism seems to be encouraged by the view that the ideal of objectivity implies absolutism and dogmatism, ideas which have now become commonplace in contemporary sociology of knowledge. To think, however, that we have made some progress towards sorting out what is true from what is false is not to reject the possibility that our claims to knowledge may be undermined. We remain open-minded, and are properly so described, because we are willing to amend our views if there is good reason to do so.

A tenacious defence of a position is also perfectly compatible with open-mindedness, though Kuhn has done much to obscure this possibility.[5] It is a mistake to assume, as Kuhn tends to do, that the open-minded individual must pursue every false but attractive idea which turns up. One goes on defending and articulating a position, but with an eye open for difficulties and problems. We cannot, I think, spell out context-free criteria for open-minded behavior. Sometimes, we will expect an individual to try to think up alternatives to his or her position. At other times, it will be enough to deal with the objections raised by others. Even here, consideration might have to be deferred until important work is completed. Identifying open-minded individuals is notoriously difficult, but we should not saddle ourselves in advance with confused notions such as the view that resistance to an idea automatically implies closed-mindedness. It is vital that we inquire into the reasons for the resistance. We need to look behind particular bits of behavior to see what they reveal about the person's thinking.

Popular stereotypes may tend to associate open-mindedness with particular subjects, but as a general attitude it can be brought to bear on any subject whatever. Many teachers who profess to support the ideal of open-mindedness seem ready to regard it as someone else's concern. If our subject, however, is based on evidence and reason, then error and fallacy can enter in. The open-minded attitude is that of being prepared to entertain this possibility. It may be that some areas of inquiry are peculiarly liable to bias and prejudice, but this simply means that we must be more vigilant. Open-mindedness cannot guarantee that we will arrive at true beliefs; it may even lead us to abandon true beliefs through error. But anyone who is concerned to discover truth must recognize a presumption in favor of open-mindedness.

Even if we agree to disagree about the relative importance of open-mindedness as an aim of education, however, the conceptual confusion surrounding the idea makes it enormously difficult to indicate what recognition of this aim would entail by way of classroom practice. Appropriate practice demands sound theory, and our theoretical views about open-mindedness are confused. Practical recommendations make various questionable assumptions about the nature of open-mindedness and its connection with other attitudes and states of mind. If we do not properly understand open-mindedness, we are likely to recommend inappropriate, or even incompatible, strategies in its name. The purpose of this discussion is to review certain practical suggestions for demonstrating and/or promoting open-mindedness in the classroom.

The Teacher's Language

It has recently been argued that the use of the word "prove" and its derivatives in teaching science demonstrates a lack of open-mindedness, and that such words should be banned from the science classroom.[6] Presumably, if we think the proposal to institute a ban fanciful, the suggestion could be interpreted as a recommendation in favor of self-restraint. Although Richard Moore limits his claim about the word "prove" to the context of science teaching, and even makes an exception in the case of mathematics, it could readily be taken to apply to the use of similar words in other subjects. Examples might be words such as *definitive* with respect to interpretation in literature, or *decisive* in respect to evidence in history, and so on.

These extensions are plausible because Moore's recommendation reflects a more general concern that certain words imply *absolute truth*, a condition of finality which puts a halt to further inquiry. Now since open-mindedness involves a willingness to revise one's ideas in the light of evidence and argument, it would seem at first that such words do demonstrate a lack of open-mindedness on the part of the teacher. Moore draws upon familiar points in the philosophy of science to show that the kinds of propositions which are crucial in scientific theory cannot be established or confirmed beyond all possibility of revision. Scientific hypotheses can perhaps be corroborated as they continue to resist efforts to falsify them, but the possibility of falsification necessarily remains.

Moore does not comment on the word *disprove*, and it may be that he would make an exception for this derivative term. After all, it might be said, there is an important logical difference between verification and falsification in science, since a single counter-instance can accomplish what a thousand confirming cases cannot. It may be then that Moore would agree with Pasteur's advice that we should try to prove ourselves wrong rather than right. It needs to be noted, however, that the idea of *absolute* disproof is also offensive to open-mindedness, since refutations and falsifications can be challenged.

For similar reasons, the notion of absolute proof needs to be challenged wherever it appears, even in mathematics where Moore is prepared to allow an exception.[7] Despite the fact that we are dealing with demonstrative reasoning in mathematics, it is clear that deductive argument, like any other, is capable of being conducted well or badly. Second thoughts may be necessary. Claims in mathematics are not subject to defeat in the same way as empirical claims, but they may be shown to be faulty nonetheless.

The fundamental question, however, is whether or not the notion of proof implies the absoluteness rightly rejected by Moore. Let us recall here that Hume thought it useful to distinguish between proofs and probabilities in empirical matters so as to mark off those claims which leave "no room for doubt or opposition."[8] That phrase might seem to smack of dogmatism, but it might also be no more than an honest indication of our *present* view that we see no room for doubt or objection. The notion of proof does not imply that the claim has been placed beyond the bounds of possible challenge. The concept of proof indicates the conviction that the claim will not be overturned. Often such confidence turns out to have been misplaced. Even when it remains intact, however, it is never *unintelligible* that counterevidence should arise to defeat that claim. Our readiness to say that the matter is proven does not imply, and need not suggest, an unwillingness to admit that the proof has run into difficulties subsequently. It reflects our belief that this will not occur.

Contrary to Moore, it is not the *use* of the word "prove," or words such as "definitive" and "decisive," which demonstrate a lack of open-mindedness, but rather the *way* in which these words are employed by the teacher. Certainly, there is a serious threat to open-mindedness if they are used with that tone of finality which indicates that "there's an end on't." Equally clearly, the words may not be employed with this implication at all. One moral here is that we cannot enter a classroom and simply determine that the teacher is closed-minded by checking off the use of certain words on a list. A check-list can, of course, be useful if appealed to intelligently and with a sense of judgment.[9] There is always the danger, however, that the difficult task of contextual judgment will be replaced by the appeal to readily measurable behavioral data. The teacher's language is an important clue, but it remains necessary to determine the attitudes which the language represents. These cannot be read off in the straightforward manner suggested by Moore.[10]

The Teacher's Stance

Open-mindedness is important in teaching any subject at any level,[11] but a critical test of the teacher's open-mindedness occurs in the context of teaching controversial material. It is this context which has occasioned much of the debate in recent years, a particular stimulus being the work of the Humanities Curriculum Project.[12] In a recent discussion of teaching controversial issues, Robert Stradling has maintained that "the litmus test of teaching ought to be whether pupils who complete the course or unit of lessons on issues are more likely to question their own and other people's assumptions and points of view."[13] In other words, a crucial measure of success is the extent to which the students become more open-minded.

Stradling is no absolutist, and he has some sensible criticisms to make of those who see their own preferred approach as *the* method to adopt invariably. His own view is that "it simply is not possible to lay down hard and fast rules about teaching controversial issues which could be applied at all times."[14] A number of relevant factors have to be considered, from the age and ability of the students to the prevailing classroom climate. Advocates of particular approaches need to recognize that their preferences are no more than useful methods in particular circumstances. They are not sacrosanct educational principles.

All this is eminently sensible, and chimes in very well with Robin Barrow's recent reminder that the contribution that teachers make "has to be based on their own judgment of the situation in which they find themselves."[15] More-over, on the various models of teaching which he selects for discussion, namely (i) a balanced approach, (ii) an objective approach, (iii) procedural neutrality, and (iv) commitment, Stradling raises a number of pertinent questions likely to foster that "greater conceptual grip on education" that Barrow has deemed so essential. Do we know what a balanced approach involves?[16] Is objectivity possible in view of the bias present in sources of information? What hard evidence is there in favor of procedural neutrality? Is committed teaching invariably appropriate? It is fair to say, I think, that Stradling's discussion offers some down-to-earth, practical advice concerning the promotion of open-mindedness in the classroom.[17] It is vital that teachers recognize that there is no magic solution to this problem.

One difficulty, however, with the recommendation that these four approaches be regarded as no more than "useful methods for teaching some issues in some circumstances" is simply that they are not all *methods* in the same sense. Stradling has run together in a confusing way a teacher's *stance* and a teacher's *standards*. He criticizes philosophers for having gone on to suggest suitable teaching methods on the basis of conceptual analysis, but this criticism misses the mark. Philosophers have argued that whatever methods are employed, certain criteria must be satisfied; or they have tried to show that recommendations for or against particular methods cannot be based exclusively on conceptual grounds.

Procedural neutrality is most clearly a method in the traditional sense, for it spelled out a pattern of behavior distinct from instruction, Socratic questions, and other techniques. By contrast, the teacher was to be "a neutral and relatively recessive chairman."[18] Stradling is surely right to insist that there is no evidence to show, and no reason to believe, that procedural neutrality is always appropriate. In retrospect, it is hard to see why it was not simply presented as one, possibly useful, approach.[19] One reason perhaps was the conceptual mistake of believing that commitment could not *in principle* represent open-mindedness, and, therefore, could not possibly help to promote it. Empirical confirmation of the claim was thought to be otiose.

Though not in itself a method in the same way as procedural neutrality, commitment resembles it in being a stance which the teacher can adopt. The teacher may have commitments which he or she chooses to conceal in order to take up a neutral pose. On the other hand, the teacher may choose to defend positions which he or she believes in, or those which the teacher believes ought to be given a defence in the classroom. In either of these ways, the teacher will take up and champion a position, and there is no reason to believe that this is always reprehensible. It is equally clear that it is not invariably desirable. With respect to both neutrality and commitment, there are indeed no hard and fast rules.

It is a mistake, however, to put balance and objectivity in the same category as neutrality and commitment. Whereas the latter are stances which are sometimes appropriate, the former are standards which are always relevant and significant in determining one's classroom practice. They are particularly pertinent in the context of fostering open-mindedness, for they represent ideals which open-minded teachers are concerned to try to satisfy.[20] The notion of a balanced treatment is related to the ideal of impartiality where a full and fair presentation is sought.[21] Objectivity is essentially related to the ideal of truth where evidence and argument are crucial. These ideals as such are not context-dependent, and it can only confuse matters to suggest that their value is relative in the manner of neutrality or commitment. What is true, of course, is that what will count as respecting these standards will vary from one situation to another, and here again good judgment is indispensable. Even when the teacher decides that a dose of flagrant bias is called for,[22] this can only be because the ideals of objectivity and impartiality have been lost sight of by the students. Here, paradoxically, bias might count as balancing the situation.

The Subject Taught

It has long been part of the conventional wisdom that individual subjects have a special contribution to make to the development of particular educational outcomes. Thus art is said to promote creativity, philosophy is linked with critical thinking, literature is connected with discrimination, and so on. There are two main problems with these all-too-tempting ideas. First, it is not clear why *each* of these subjects could not contribute something to the development of *each* of these abilities. Second, it is not clear that any *one* subject can develop a transferable, general ability. The disastrous consequences of the general assumption is that teachers begin to feel that the promotion of certain educational outcomes is *someone else's* responsibility. Thus, with respect to a host of ideals such as duty, responsibility, justice, kindness, tolerance, and good faith, we are told that "science would not appear to be a particularly fruitful field in which to pursue these objectives."[23]

If science teachers disclaim responsibility in these areas, and fortunately not all do, they stake out a claim for a special link between the study of science and the development of open-mindedness. That this view is rather taken for granted becomes clear when we find the link being asserted in passing, when the explicit subject is not the aims of education at all. In a review of a recent book about the nature of science, we come across the following:

> "But also, while more open-minded than most people, scientists are – again because of their training – less gullible about things scientific than the general population."[24]

Our confidence in the latter judgment might be greater if the former were not precisely that sort of unsupported generalization which scientists, because of their training, ought to be wary of making.

Lest we dismiss this quotation as illustrating nothing more than the prejudice of a scientist, we should recognize that similar views permeate a great deal of thinking about the role of science in education. First, there is the fact that certain important work in the history and sociology of science has come about as a response to what has been perceived as the stereotype of the scientist as open-minded.[25] Second, influential philosophers have explicitly encouraged the link in question. Bertrand Russell, for example, held that "absence of finality is the essence of the scientific spirit. The beliefs of the man of science are therefore tentative and undogmatic."[26] Finally, we might point to a tendency in the writings of those who deal with the value and aims of a scientific education to speak of open-mindedness as a *scientific* or *science-related* attitude,[27] suggesting an exclusive connection with science. Hence, it might be thought that one very practical way of promoting open-mindedness would be to ensure that students are exposed to science.

There are many reasons, however, to be concerned about such a recommendation, notwithstanding that open-mindedness *is* an important value in science. First, the exclusive nature of the claim is simply mistaken. Open-mindedness is equally important in the study of history, literature, mathematics, and philosophy.[28] The effect of delegating this responsibility to the science teacher is simply to reduce drastically what ought to be a concerted effort on the part of all teachers. Second, although open-mindedness is an attitude, and consequently transferable *in principle* from one area to another, we cannot just assume that there will *in fact* be such transference from science to other matters. It may, for example, be more difficult to adopt this attitude in political, moral, and religious matters, and this would suggest the need for attention to open-mindedness in all those subjects which bear on such issues. Third, it is a mistake to assume that the teaching of science will necessarily reflect an open-minded attitude. Scientists are not invariably open-minded,[29] and many, following Kuhn,[30] believe that there is much to be said for dogmatism in science and science teaching. Even those who believe in the ideal of open-mindedness may fail to communicate this to their students.

There can be little comfort then in the mere fact that students are studying science, or any other particular subject for that matter. What we need to know is *how* science or whatever is being taught. Teachers need to recognize that open-mindedness is possible and desirable in teaching any subject matter worthy of inclusion in an educational curriculum. To the extent that a subject is understood to exclude open-minded inquiry, a pseudoscience for example, that is sufficient reason in an educational context for not *pursuing* it, although it will be worth learning that and why it fails to be a science.[31]

The Classroom Atmosphere

Just as the possibility of open-minded reflection about certain topics is much greater in some societies than others, so too the atmosphere in a classroom can inhibit or facilitate open-mindedness. This point is well recognized, but again it has given rise to a number of doubtful recommendations.

Herbert Kohl, for example, set out to characterize openness in the classroom,[32] and produced what he called a practical guide to a new way of teaching. Openness and open-mindedness are by no means equivalent, of course, but Kohl's general criticism of authoritarian classrooms makes it reasonable to assume that open-mindedness is an important aspect of his conception of the open classroom. Kohl's first chapter entitled "Beginning the School Year" is devoted to suggestions for creating an open atmosphere, and it advises that "a teacher has to learn to go with the class, to respond to their desire to learn about things and not cut off their enthusiasm in the service of getting through the curriculum."[33]

There is, surely, an important truth here. Kohl is speaking of the need to be flexible, to avoid rigidity, and to be prepared to make some serious interactive decisions.[34] It will be difficult to demonstrate our open-mindedness if we are locked into a pre-determined curriculum. And yet Kohl's advice is not adequate: it blurs the difference between an open-minded atmosphere and a free-wheeling one. We can see this if we look closely at what Kohl has to say in the same paragraph about the objectionable character of authoritarian imposition. It is arbitrary. This is a crucial objection in an educational context where reason is paramount, but it applies equally to the suggestion that the teacher "go with the class." An arbitrary jump from studying motion in physics to motion in dance, to use one of Kohl's own examples, may or may not be appropriate, and we must not assume that if we are open-minded we must go along. In following up such associations, what is being learned of educational value?

Some years ago, Hirst and Peters laid down the challenge when they wondered "what is gained by organizing a project on hands concerned with physiology, the conditions of employment of factory hands, and the religious significance of the laying on of hands,"[35] and I am not aware that any answer has been forthcoming. Our doubts ought to be greater when we are speaking not of a planned project but simply of pursuing an idea which pops up on the spot. Open-mindedness is not shown by the weather-vane mentality, and once again we see how crucial it is for teachers to possess a clear concept here. Kohl is on somewhat safer ground when he cautions in a later book that "there are no firm guidelines to help one function with sanity and responsibility,"[36] except that if guidelines were seen as just that and no more, firmness would not be an objection.

The motivation behind the freewheeling atmosphere is clearly the threat to open-mindedness from an authoritarian teacher or curriculum. This fear also explains certain suggestions for creating a healthy atmosphere which revolve around the teacher's possession of knowledge or answers. These suggestions take a variety of forms but include the idea that the teacher should constantly remind himself that he or she is at most only another member of the discussion group,[37] and the view that when the teacher asks questions to which he or she knows the answer, an open-minded discussion will degenerate into a recitation, a quiz-show atmosphere.[38]

What is wrong here is not the idea that the quiz-show atmosphere is inimical to open-mindedness, for if students are merely trying to state or guess the correct answer, from memory or from inspiration, open-mindedness can get no grip on the situation. The problem, rather, is that a faulty notion of open-mindedness lies behind these recommendations. In the first place, having an answer does not preclude the possibility of the teacher being willing to reconsider it. Secondly, teachers may be able to indicate that they think they have an answer and still encourage the expression of a variety of viewpoints which are more than idle guesses.

The mistaken view seems to be that open-mindedness can only enter those situations where we recognize that we do not have an answer to a problem. But it is an attitude which we can adopt and display towards what we regard as the best answers now available. If we couple this mistaken view with the fashionable but independently false belief that "most of the knowledge from the arts . . . and academic disciplines that belongs in the primary and secondary school curriculum is non-controversial,"[39] one can readily see how the very ideal of open-mindedness can seem misplaced in the school curriculum. The open-minded teacher does not need to tell himself or herself that his or her knowledge is no greater than that of the student. The relevant equality is something quite different. All participants, teacher and students alike, are equally obliged to support their ideas by reason and evidence, and obliged to withdraw them in the light of decisive objections.

Concluding Comment

Those who seek to offer concrete, practical advice to teachers consistently overlook the fact that one and the same behavior, asking a question for example, can be carried out in different ways. Teachers do not all ask questions in the same spirit. A behavioral maxim blurs these differences, and in doing so helps to promote an erroneous view of open-mindedness itself.

It is clear that those like Stradling and Norris who have argued against hard and fast rules and "quick-fix" solutions are on the right lines. Although the proposals considered here have been found to be unsatisfactory, this does not mean that the outcome is entirely negative. Teachers *must* learn to develop their own judgment but if that is all we can say it is not very helpful. What is needed is for teachers to see how intuitively plausible suggestions rest ultimately on an inadequate grasp of what open-mindedness involves. Clarity here is vital if teachers are to hope to present themselves as open-minded individuals to their students.

The discussion here has shown how open-mindedness does not demand that we abandon confidence in our claims to knowledge. The point is rather that our confidence must not turn into an *a priori* contempt towards counter-claims. Furthermore, if there is no one way available to promote the aims, there are relevant standards such as objectivity and impartiality which can serve to guide judgment. It is not a step in the direction of open-mindedness to have a cavalier attitude towards these, though we need to remember that in any absolute sense they may be unattainable in practice. Teachers are not likely to make even an effort in this direction, however, if they fall victim to the idea that the scope of open-mindedness is restricted to a particular subject-matter. In view of the fact that it is a difficult ideal to aspire to, it would be easy to succumb to the view that it is not one's concern at all. Finally, we should bear in mind that our desire to create an open-minded atmosphere in the classroom could be frustrated by simplistic suggestions which only manage to convey a distorted sense of what open-mindedness is and what it demands.

Notes

1. John Dewey, *Democracy and Education,* New York: Macmillan, 1916: 175.

2. See Paul Kurtz, "Debunking, neutrality and scepticism in science," *The Skeptical Inquirer 8*, 3, 1984: 239-246.

3. See my discussion in *Open-mindedness and Education,* op cit.

4. See John White, *The Aims of Education Restated*, London: Routledge and Kegan Paul, 1982.

5. Thomas S. Kuhn, "The function of dogma in scientific research," in A. C. Crombie (ed.), *Scientific Change*, London: Heinemann, 1963: 347-69.

6. Richard W. Moore, "Open-mindedness and proof," *School Science and Mathematics 82*, 6, 1982: 478-80.

7. This point is also noted by Stephen P. Norris in "Cynicism, dogmatism, relativism and scepticism: Can all these be avoided?" *School Science and Mathematics 84*, 6, 1984: 484-494. See p. 488. Norris, however, seems too ready to accept without question Kuhn's characterization of the normal scientist as "dogmatic." In general, however, his criticisms of Moore are sound.

8. David Hume, *An Inquiry Concerning the Principles of Morals*, 1751, Section VI, footnote 1.

9. For more on this, see chapter 7 in this collection on "Alleged bias in children's books."

10. It is also worth noting that students ought to be learning that many "proofs" have been relegated to the museum of ideas. This should serve to counteract any misleading connotation.

11. See, for example, my "Open-mindedness in elementary education," in *Elementary School Journal 83*, 3, 1983: 212-219. Reprinted in William Hare and John P. Portelli (eds.), *Philosophy of Education: Introductory Readings*, op cit. For a related discussion, see chapter 5 of the present collection.

12. See Lawrence Stenhouse, "The Humanities curriculum project: The rationale," *Theory into Practice 10*, 3, June 1971: 154-162. The philosophical discussion includes: my paper, "Controversial issues and the teacher," *High School Journal 57*, 2, 1973: 51-60, reprinted in my *Controversies in Teaching* London, Ont.: Althouse Press, 1985. Also: Charles Bailey, "Neutrality and rationality in teaching," in D. Bridges and P. Scrimshaw (eds.), *Values and Authority in Schools,* London: Hodder and Stoughton, 1975: 121-134. And: R.F. Dearden, "Controversial issues and the curriculum," *Journal of Curriculum Studies 13*, 1, 1981: 37-44. Reprinted in William Hare and John P. Portelli (eds.), *Philosophy of Education: Introductory Readings*, op. cit. For further discussion of the Humanities Curriculum Project, see chapter 8 of the present collection.

13. Robert Stradling, "The teaching of controversial issues: An evaluation," *Educational Review 36*, 2, 1984: 128.

14. Stradling, op. cit.: 126.

15. Robin Barrow, "Teacher judgement and teacher effectiveness," *Journal of Educational Thought 18*, 2, 1984: 81.

16. cf. Robert Dearden, "Balance and coherence: Some curricular principles in recent reports," *Cambridge Journal of Education 11*, 2, 1981: 107-118.

17. Stradling never employs the term "open-mindedness," but there is no doubt at all that this concept is central to his discussion.

18. Stenhouse, op. cit.: 157.

19. That it was not is clear, despite disclaimers. On this, see my *Open-mindedness and Education*, op. cit.: 67.

20. See Alan Montefiore, *Neutrality and Impartiality,* London: Cambridge University Press, 1975: 21.

21. See Brenda Cohen, *Means and Ends in Education*, London: Allen and Unwin, 1983: 90.

22. See Bernard Crick, "On Bias," *Teaching Politics 1*, 1, 1972: 3-12.

23. R. A. R. Tricker, *The Contribution of Science to Education,* London: Mills and Boon Limited, 1967: 6.

24. George Abell, review of *Science and Unreason* in *The Skeptical Inquirer 7*, 2, 1982-83: 65.

25. See Thomas S. Kuhn, *The Structure of Scientific Revolutions*, Chicago: University of Chicago Press, 1962. And: Bernard Barber, "Resistance by scientists to scientific discovery," *Science 134*, 1961: 596-602. Reprinted in Bernard Barber and Walter Hirsch (eds.), *The Sociology of Science*, New York: Free Press of Glencoe, 1962: 539-556.

26. Bertrand Russell, *Education and the Social Order,* London: Unwin Books, 1967: 15.

27. See, for example, Richard E. Haney, "The development of scientific attitudes," in Edward Victor and Marjorie S. Lerner (eds.), *Readings in Science Education for the Elementary School*, New York: Macmillan, 1971: 69-76. Also, Morris Kline, "The liberal education values of science," in ibid.:15-19. See also, Graham W. F. Orpwood and Jean-Pascal Souque, *Science Education in Canadian Schools Vol. 1*, Ottawa: Science Council of Canada, 1984: 64.

28. cf. Israel Scheffler, *Science and Subjectivity*, Indianapolis: Bobbs-Merrill, 1967: 2. Scheffler makes the point in connection with the ideal of objectivity.

29. See William Broad and Nicholas Wade, *Betrayers of the Truth*, New York: Simon Schuster, 1982.

30. Thomas S. Kuhn, "The function of dogma in scientific research," in A.C. Crombie (ed.), *Scientific Change*, London: Heinemann, 1963: 347-369.

31. See Mario Bunge, "What is pseudoscience?" *The Skeptical Inquirer 9*, 1, 1984: 34-46.

32. Herbert R. Kohl, *The Open Classroom*, New York: Vintage Books, 1969.

33. Ibid.: 31.

34. I have defended the importance of this in my "Standards as a threat to open-mindedness," *European Journal of Teacher Education 5*, 3, 1982: 133-145. See also my *In Defence of Open-mindedness,* op cit.

56 *Attitudes in Teaching and Education*

35. P.H. Hirst and R.S. Peters, *The Logic of Education,* op cit.: 71.

36. Herbert R. Kohl, *On Teaching,* New York: Bantam Books, 1977: 101.

37. John Walton, *Toward Better Teaching in the Secondary School,* Boston: Allyn and Bacon, 1966: 159.

38. J. T. Dillon, "Research on questioning and discussion," *Educational Leadership* *42,* 3, 1984: 50-56.

39. Donald Vandenberg, *Human Rights in Education,* New York: Philosophical Library, 1983: 255.

4
Open-mindedness in Moral Education

Three fashionable approaches to moral education are examined to see how far they satisfy the ideal of open-mindedness. It seems clear that values clarification, situation ethics, and critical issues all seek to avoid indoctrination and, in different ways, present an alternative to traditional moral instruction with its emphasis on absolute moral rules. In stressing the autonomy of the individual, in denouncing prefabricated rules, and in promoting discussion of vexed questions, a clear concern for open-mindedness can be detected. It is argued, however, that an inadequate account of open-mindedness pervades these approaches. Moral education would benefit from a positive account of open-mindedness; it is not enough merely to avoid the grosser forms of indoctrination.

Introduction

It would perhaps be surprising if approaches to moral education were not simplified and sloganized. Not being sure, on the one hand, that morality can be taught at all and knowing, on the other, the tremendous practical problems involved in making the attempt to teach it, it would be tempting to try to avoid the messy business altogether. Equally clear, however, is the fact that failure to act will also have serious moral consequences, and thus we are driven to find some acceptable approach. In this uncertain condition, we are easy prey for well-marketed strategies which appear to offer solutions to the major problems of moral education.

In recent years, the central problem has been seen as that of avoiding indoctrination. Both the notion of education itself and that of being a fully moral agent require that a person be able to think for himself or herself. Indoctrination, which seeks to produce a closed mind, is incompatible with this requirement. There may be doubts about how far open-mindedness should be taken in the context of morality,[1] but it is widely agreed that a measure of open-mindedness is an essential aspect of any serious approach to moral education. In short, people need to be able to make up their own minds about moral issues based on consideration of evidence and argument, and should be prepared to revise their thinking if confronted with relevant objections and difficulties.

An open-minded attitude is quite compatible with having principles and convictions. What is required is not that we regard all moral positions as equally valid, but that we regard our own as subject to revision in the light of critical reflection. Moreover, regarding our moral views as subject to revision does not mean that we adopt a sceptical attitude towards them. The test of open-mindedness is rather whether or not we are prepared to *entertain* doubts about our views. Sometimes, when we are open-minded, we will not have made up our minds on a moral issue, but the link with neutrality is not a logically necessary one. A person can be open-minded about his or her moral views in the sense that they are potentially alterable as a result of reflection. When we are trying to form a moral view on some issue, open-mindedness is shown in our willingness to consider all relevant evidence and arguments as impartially and objectively as possible.[2]

Three approaches to moral education which have been enormously influential of late can readily be seen as attempts to satisfy different aspects of open-mindedness in the context of moral education. (1) *Values clarification* essentially seeks to prevent the values of other people being imposed. Moralizing and propaganda are firmly rejected. (2) *Situation ethics* abandons the notion of hard and fast rules in morality and attempts to determine what one ought to do in particular situations bearing in mind that "circumstances alter cases." (3) *Critical issues* challenge the view that morality is common-sense, clear-cut, and obvious, and this approach encourages the idea that morality is controversial and problematic, requiring hard thinking.

It seems clear that, in different ways, these three methods attempt to grapple with the problem of moral indoctrination, and their proponents would readily admit this motivation. Certainly, old-style moral instruction, with its emphasis on absolute moral rules as definitive and without exception, fell far short of the ideal of open-mindedness. We need to ask, however, how far these fashionable replacements are adequate and appropriate.

Values Clarification[3]

The theory and methodology of values clarification represents a response to what is perceived as a pervasive confusion and uncertainty about values, particularly among the young. The sources of confusion include the conflicting influences children receive, the pluralistic nature of contemporary society, the changing character of the modern family, and the inconsistency between professed ideals and actual practice in everyday life. The proposal is that, as the proponents put it, "each person has to wrest his own values from the available array,"[4] and dozens of pedagogical strategies are outlined so that teachers may assist students in this process. The ideal outcome is one in which an individual freely chooses, prizes, and acts on his or her own set of values.

The numerous strategies include games, exercises, activities, and stories which create or suggest situations in which students are encouraged to think out what their own values are. For example, the Rank Order strategy asks students to place various alternatives in order of importance. If one were given $500, for example, would one save it, give it to charity, or buy something for oneself? The Unfinished Sentences strategy invites students to complete some such opening remark as "If I had 24 hours to live . . ." or "Secretly I wish . . ."

The Taking a Stand strategy involves the selection of a controversial issue by the teacher and/or students and having the students write a suitable slogan. Unless a strategy deliberately excludes critical discussion, as in the case of brainstorming, students are also involved in explaining and defending their choices, and much is made of the virtue of attending to the views of others.

There is a good deal, surely, in both the general conception and the methodology of values clarification for the defender of open-mindedness to endorse and welcome. First, we find a serious concern about the problems of indoctrination and coercion in the area of values. Emphasis is placed on free choice and personal decision. Second, a serious choice is understood to involve awareness of a range of alternatives which are given careful consideration. Here decisions are made in the light of what can be said for and against the various alternatives rather than as a result of preconceived notions. Finally, we might note the attempt to open up the field of discussion to include many issues and topics often deemed taboo.[5]

Similarly, as concerns the method and its implementation, open-mindedness appears, first, in the rejection of moralizing where a particular set of values is dogmatically inculcated. Second, there is an appreciation of the need for a certain atmosphere in the classroom if open-mindedness is to flourish. So-called "discussions," for example, can soon degenerate into purely defensive argumentation.[6] Third, there is a recognition of various ways in which unconscious bias can confound sincere efforts at open-minded teaching, and a number of suggestions for uncovering and dealing with this problem are offered.[7] Finally, there seems to be a genuine attempt to identify methods which will allow students to think out their own position, to respond to open-ended, non-judgmental questions, to listen to the views of other people, and to consider possibilities which might have been altogether neglected. All of this is conducive to open-minded reflection on moral issues.

In view of these many positive features, it might seem mere carping to mention some reservations. Unfortunately, these are sufficiently serious that values clarification cannot be viewed as an adequate model of open-minded moral education. In the first place, any approach to values which is genuinely open-minded must embrace the possibility that our values need to be *revised* because they are inadequate. To be open-minded, after all, includes being willing to revise or even abandon a position in the light of counter-evidence and counter-argument. But this is a possibility which the approach, with its stress on clarification, never takes seriously. The objective is not to revise our moral views but simply to make clearer what they are and what they entail.

Secondly, and what serves to explain the preceding position, it is not clear that the notion of an inadequate moral view has any status in the values clarification conception. We are told that "teachers might well see themselves as obliged to support the idea that every individual is entitled to the views he has and to the values that he holds,"[8] and we are urged to be deeply suspicious of approaches to moral education which attempt to foster the "right" values. If the notion of truth has no purchase in this area, however, then the notion of open-mindedness is also irrelevant since it is tied to evidence and argument. And if one moral view is no better than another, there would seem to be no point in changing one's moral views at all. None of this is to say, to echo Joel Feinberg, that we need to think in terms of proofs and refutations in morality. But we do need to reject the view that all value judgments are equally acceptable. Through discussion and reflection we hope to arrive at more satisfactory moral views.

Thirdly, the attack on moralizing is misunderstood to constitute a critique of moral instruction in general. Those who support values clarification find that all traditional approaches to moral education "have the air of indoctrination, with some merely more subtle than others."[9] The complaint is that reason seems to be lost. This would be a fatal criticism if true, but it is impossible to see, however, how it could apply to the traditional approach which the proponents of values clarification themselves characterize as: "Persuading and convincing by presenting arguments and reasons for this or that set of values and by pointing to the fallacies and pitfalls of other sets of values."[10] Here, surely, the complaint cannot be that reason is lost, only that it might be lost sight of in practice. And any approach runs this risk. The point is that rational persuasion is not itself incompatible with open-minded teaching. Ironically, it is values clarification which appears to have abandoned reason in adopting the view that there is no rational way of discriminating between rival moral views.

Fourthly, although the enemy in the field is said to be indoctrination, and hence closed-mindedness, the positive ideal which values clarification actually represents is tolerance rather than open-mindedness. The language employed makes this plain. Teachers must "open up decisions" and create "freedom to choose." They "cannot dictate to children what their values should be." It is even possible that children will choose not to develop values, and "it is the teacher's responsibility to support this choice also." A clarifying response from the teacher should be "permissive and stimulating, but not insistent." Teachers need to maintain "that accepting atmosphere" and a "non-judgmental approach."[11] All this speaks of tolerance not open-mindedness. Tolerance, if distinguished from permissiveness, is an important ideal, but there is no implication that the tolerant person will be in any way open-minded. In setting an example of tolerance in the classroom, the teacher is not thereby setting an example of open-mindedness, and one potential counter to indoctrination is neglected.[12]

Despite the fact then that values clarification incorporates certain features which are conducive to the promotion of open-mindedness, the approach does not in fact amount to an example of this ideal in practice, and, indeed, given its relativistic underpinnings, cannot amount to this. Moreover, in using the term "moralizing" so loosely, it creates an unwarranted prejudice against other potentially valuable approaches. There is finally the point that in pretending to an absolute neutrality, when in fact numerous values are embedded in the approach, there is the danger that a rather spurious openness is involved.[13]

Situation Ethics[14]

At first glance, situation ethics would appear to be the epitome of an open-minded approach to morality, for it involves turning away from "fixed principles, closed systems, and pretended absolutes and origins."[15] It is vital that people take into account the particular features of the situation or context in which the moral decision arises, and not be "encumbered with a whole apparatus of prefabricated rules and regulations."[16] Certainly, if moral rules are going to dictate a decision, there can arise no question for open-minded reflection about what that decision ought to be.

The existence of moral rules does permit a limited degree of open-mindedness, partly because moral rules sometimes conflict and reflection is needed, and partly because it may not be clear that a particular rule applies in a certain case. Situation ethics, on the other hand, rejects the view that moral decision-making is merely a matter of trying to determine which moral rule applies in a particular situation. It also takes the view that "circumstances can even alter principles,"[17] thus recognizing that general principles may need to be revised in the light of specific judgments.[18]

The distinction drawn between rules and principles is also likely to commend itself to those who defend open-mindedness. Situation ethics discards the notion of hard and fast rules in ethics, maintaining that there are only "rules of thumb."[19] Thus, the idea of a fixed and absolute moral code is abandoned, and a more flexible and thoughtful approach substituted. But general principles, sometimes referred to as maxims, are not discounted. Indeed, "the situationist enters into every decision-making situation fully armed with the ethical maxims of his community and its heritage."[20] The suggestion then that situation ethics dismisses the accumulated wisdom of the past, or even that it is inconsistent with the very idea of moral education, is wide of the mark, or so it would seem.

Although situation ethics is essentially a conception of ethics rather than a methodology of moral education, one can readily infer methodological implications. These too appear to chime in well with the ideal of open-mindedness. Clearly, there would be no dogmatic and doctrinaire statement of a moral code to be blindly accepted. Children would be expected and encouraged to think out their own moral position in the light of relevant features of the situations considered. The teacher would be viewed as a guide rather than as one who lays down the law. Moral education would not simply be a matter of clarifying what one happens to think, but of trying to decide what one ought to do given the facts of the situation.

Despite these commendable aspects which have played a part in shifting contemporary approaches to moral education away from indoctrination, situation ethics has some serious shortcomings from the standpoint of open-mindedness. First, although there is an express repudiation of relativism,[21] and an equally clear rejection of intuitionism,[22] it is not at all clear how open-minded reflection is supposed to work. Certainly, some decisions are to be viewed as superior to others, and these are not supposed to be presented in any kind of mysterious insight. Exactly how they are to be determined, however, is quite vague. The fundamental guiding principle, the only absolute principle acknowledged in situation ethics, is love or *agape*. Apart from numerous examples and cases, however, we have no way of knowing how to apply this principle in particular cases. Clearly, it is often controversial what love requires. Again, it is by no means clear that the principle of love never conflicts with any other principle. The view that "love alone when well served is always good and right in every situation"[23] demands an account of "well served" if it is not to be dismissed as a mere tautology. We are told that we are to act in a certain way "if the situation calls for it,"[24] but criteria as vague and empty as this inevitably mean that we fall back on intuition.

Second, there is the erroneous assumption that open-mindedness precludes having firm and deep-rooted moral convictions. Situation ethics "repudiates any attempt to anticipate or prescribe real-life decisions in their existential particularity,"[25] but moral principles do attempt to do this and rightly so. Unless we have a firm commitment to certain moral principles, we will lack the sorts of dispositions which lead us to do certain things without hesitation.[26] We know from experience that certain sorts of actions are more likely to produce good results, and it is useful to have a strong inclination to act in these ways. This does not mean that the principles in question can never be examined or challenged, but this is different from the view that they are up for discussion anew in every case. Situation ethics maintains that we are to be "armed" with principles and maxims, but the emphasis would seem to be on awareness rather than commitment.

Third, there is the practical objection that every case cannot in fact be minutely examined to determine our moral obligation. And there is no need for this, since it is often clear that detailed examination would cost more than any expectable benefit. Situation ethics is open to the objection that it requires an excessive and unreasonable attention to the details of each and every situation calling for a moral decision. We are told that it is doubtful if situations ever have enough in common to support more than a cautious generalization,[27] and the view that "every case is like every other case, and no two cases are alike" is cheerfully cited.[28] Open-mindedness, on the other hand, does not require this attitude. It is enough that we are prepared to revise a view in the light of serious difficulties. If no two cases really were alike, it is hard to see how we could learn from past experience or what the notion of moral education would come to. Other practical limitations inherent in situation ethics include the fact that there is not always time to deal with each situation as if it were unique, and the danger of error if we decide to form our own view contrary to well-established principles. The "utter openness" which situationists are fond of defending,[29] can become nothing more than empty-minded flexibility. William Barclay says that if we were saints, situation ethics would be perfect.[30] It is clear, however, that, in addition to saintliness, archangelic wisdom would also be needed.[31]

Finally, we should note that situation ethics has remarkably little positive advice to offer on moral education. It clearly opposes a legalistic approach which amounts to inculcating absolute rules, and harsh criticism is directed at the very idea of a moral code. There is an important distinction between a code and a set of guidelines, but situation ethics, with its emphasis on the tentative and the contingent, might have taken more seriously something like Descartes' idea of a provisional moral code.[32] In making the contrast sharply between an ethics based on a code and one which is not, situation ethics ignores the crucial matter of the *spirit* in which a code is passed on and acquired. Descartes declared his intention of changing his moral opinions as soon as he could find better ones,[33] and children can be encouraged to develop similar attitudes. At the same time, until one's moral judgment develops, it is manifestly useful to have a clear set of rules.

Values clarification, with its emphasis on discussion and examination, is perhaps more likely to foster a recognition that certain cases have important features in common, and that a decision in one case commits one to a similar decision in the other case. It is no mark of open-mindedness to resist the claims of universalizability. On the other hand, situation ethics gives much needed attention to the idea of revising moral rules and principles in the light of relevant facts and arguments, and this is an aspect of open-mindedness which is all but ignored in values clarification.

Critical Issues[34]

The dominant approach to moral education since the late 1960s until quite recently has been one which has focused on moral dilemmas, controversial questions, and critical, public issues. It would be a mistake, of course, to think in terms of a single, monolithic model, but there is enough in common to justify a general appraisal. The common features include: a rejection of the view that moral education involves the acquisition of a "bag of virtues" like honesty and kindness; a belief that moral education must concentrate on developing the child's ability to reason about values; an agreement that, while clarification is essential, moral education must include the question of justification and the possibility of change; and a conviction that the most suitable subject matter for stimulating moral development is the kind of issue about which serious and reasonable people hold different opinions, and for which there is no readily available answer.

A focus on controversial material helps to underline the importance of open-mindedness in the context of ethics. If serious and reasonable people disagree and no resolution is at hand, there is nothing for it but an open-minded examination of the issue and the conflicting opinions in an attempt to determine what we should think. An authoritarian, doctrinaire approach is directly challenged, for *ex hypothesi* there is no authority or doctrine in the wings to settle the conflict. Likewise, the issue will be distorted if the teacher pretends to an authority which he or she does not possess. The teacher simply does not have an authoritative answer to impart. As a result, the teacher is required to remain neutral about the substantive issue, to stimulate the development of the child's own moral judgment, and to raise provocative and challenging questions about the issues. The specific methodological recommendations vary, but the definitive, content-specific answer approach is firmly rejected.

Secondly, attention to controversial material serves to off-set the influence of the hidden curriculum, where values are soaked up as a result of the routines, practices, and general atmosphere of the school. It is now clear that indoctrination is not invariably the result of conscious intent, but sometimes results from an osmosis-like process.[35] Our minds are closed because we do not see value questions as problematic and perplexing. On the contrary, our moral views seem natural, obvious and commonsense, and in this we see the effects of what Gramsci called hegemony. Being confronted with issues which are debatable, divisive and contested is one effective way of counteracting this insidious process and of shattering our complacency.

Thirdly, if we are to do justice to the critical issue in question, it will be necessary to develop certain dispositions which are closely linked with the attitude of open-mindedness. For example, it will be crucial to listen to the various positions taken, and to do so impartially. We shall, no doubt, have to discuss various tentative answers, make certain compromises, and revise positions which seem initially attractive. We will need to have an open mind about what can be admitted as evidence with respect to the issue, since any predetermined view on this might be prejudicial. These aspects of open-mindedness are recognized by the proponents of critical issues in their call for open debate,[36] exposure to the reasoning of other students,[37] and sensitivity to what others are saying.[38]

The critical issues approach incorporates the positive aspects of values clarification and situation ethics. First, it is made abundantly clear that the process of clarification is a necessary, though by no means a sufficient, component of moral education.[39] One can make no progress on a dilemma or controversial issue until the essential features have been sorted out. Second, the case study approach recognizes the truth in situation ethics that the details and circumstances of the particular problem must be taken into account. Ready-made generalizations may come to grief in a given context. The major errors of values clarification and situation ethics, however, are avoided. There is no suggestion, for example, that all moral views are equally acceptable or that moral education is no more than discovering what one's preferences happen to be. As Stenhouse puts it, "education will always be concerned with examining criteria and establishing standards."[40] Similarly, instead of the view that we must act "as the situation requires," we encounter the idea that moral judgment draws upon universal goals and principles, and that particular moral judgments need to be assessed in the light of these. Thus the critical issues approach seeks to avoid indoctrination without embracing relativism or subjectivism.

There are, however, a number of shortcomings in the critical issues approach from the standpoint of the ideal of open-mindedness. First, open-minded teaching is too closely identified with teacher neutrality. This identification is most explicit, of course, in the work of the Schools Council in England, but it is quite evident in the Canadian Critical Issues series, and also present in the work of Kohlberg with his emphasis on Socratic questioning as the teacher's primary role.[41] The motivation is clear. It is important to avoid didacticism, moralizing and an authoritarian atmosphere in which the students try to sec-ond-guess the teacher. Certainly, teacher neutrality on the substantive issue may often be necessary and desirable. But it is quite mistaken to present neutrality as the very model of open-mindedness. A teacher can, and at times should, demonstrate his or her open-mindedness, and thereby set such an example to the students, by taking a stand in a reasonable and non-dogmatic manner, showing that the position is open for discussion and subject to revision. The danger in the teacher neutrality conception is that open-mindedness comes to be associated with fence-sitting, or with issues where we simply do not know what to think because the matter is controversial.

Second, then, we see a risk in identifying moral education exclusively with the consideration of controversial material and moral dilemmas. Apart from the fact that this approach may encourage the erroneous view that all moral issues are controversial,[42] the impression may arise that open-mindedness only comes into those situations where there is no settled view. Even well-entrenched views, however, can be challenged, can be *made* controversial, as we have seen over the past decade, for example, with the question of animal rights. Moral education needs to foster the idea that open-mindedness is a desirable attitude to adopt towards our own moral convictions, not simply to issues which we all regard as open.

Finally, the attack on the traditional "bag of virtues," such as honesty and kindness, creates the false impression that the acquisition of such traits neces-sarily amounts to indoctrination. Kohlberg seems to hold that specific content must not be built into moral education if indoctrination is to be avoided. We have seen earlier, in discussing situation ethics, that there is much to be said for acquiring various moral traits and dispositions, and here the point needs to be made that these do not compromise our open-mindedness. Certainly, Kohlberg is right to point out that agreement about the goodness of these virtues conceals a great deal of disagreement about their definitions,[43] but there is no reason why students cannot learn that the meaning of these virtues will have to be interpreted in complex situations. The "bag of virtues" versus open-mindedness is a false choice.

Concluding Comment

Although each of these approaches sets out to counter some feature of indoctrination, and thus contributes indirectly to a more open-minded conception of moral education, the fundamental problem is that each account lacks a positive conception of open-mindedness. This is perhaps not surprising since contemporary educators in general have shown more interest in characterizing indoctrination than in setting out the positive ideal.[44] The result is that, in avoiding certain forms of indoctrination, the accounts still fall short of open-mindedness. This means, unfortunately, that a necessary feature of moral education is not adequately represented. Education involves a concern for truth, and it is this concern which makes the attitude of open-mindedness a necessary aspect of the educated outlook. *A fortiori*, this is true of moral education. Those who would design an adequate program of moral education will need to give more serious attention to the ideal of open-mindedness, not merely seek to avoid the grosser errors of indoctrination.

Notes

1. I have reviewed these doubts in my *In Defence of Open-mindedness*, op. cit., ch. 3.

2. This is a brief account of open-mindedness which I have explored at length in *Open-mindedness and Education*, op. cit. and *In Defence of Open-mindedness*, op. cit. See also chapters 3 and 5 in this collection.

3. The basic texts are: Louis E. Raths, Merrill Harmin, and Sidney B. Simon, *Values and Teaching*, Columbus, Ohio: Charles E. Merrill, 1966. And, Sidney B. Simon, Leland W. Howe, and Howard Kirschenbaum, *Values Clarification: A Handbook of Practical Strategies for Teachers and Students*, New York: Hart Publishing Co., 1972.

4. Raths et al., op. cit.: 10.

5. op. cit.: 35.

6. op. cit.: 106.

7. op. cit.: 171.

8. op. cit.: 36.

9. op. cit.: 41.

10. op. cit.: 39-40.

11. These and similar remarks can be found throughout Raths et al., *Values and Teaching*, op. cit.

12. For further comments on the difference between tolerance and open-mindedness, see my "Open-mindedness in the teaching of philosophy," *Metaphilosophy 13*, 2, 1982: 165-80.

13. cf. Douglas J. Simpson and Michael J. B. Jackson, *The Teacher as Philosopher*, Toronto: Methuen, 1984: 98.

14. The central reference is Joseph Fletcher, *Situation Ethics: The New Morality*, Philadelphia: Westminster Press, 1966.

15. Fletcher, op. cit.: 43. The words are those of William James.

16. op. cit.: 18.

17. op. cit.: 29.

18. cf. Joel Feinberg, *Social Philosophy*, Englewood Cliffs, N.J.: Prentice-Hall, 1973: 3.

19. Fletcher, *Situation Ethics*, op. cit.: 36.

20. op. cit.: 26.

21. op. cit.: 44. Fletcher is prepared to call his position "principled relativism." See p. 31.

22. op. cit.: 23.

23. op. cit.: 60.

24. op. cit.: 27.

25. op. cit.: 29-30.

26. R. M. Hare, *Moral Thinking: Its Levels, Method and Point*, Oxford: Clarendon Press, 1981: 36.

27. Fletcher, *Situation Ethics*, op. cit.: 32.

28. Ibid.

29. John A. T. Robinson, *Honest To God*, London: SCM, 1963: 114.

30. William Barclay, *Ethics in a Permissive Society*, Glasgow: Fontana, 1971: 81.

31. See R. M. Hare, *Moral Thinking*, op. cit., ch. 3.

32. Descartes, *Discourse on Method*, ch. 3.

33. Descartes, letter of April, 1638, in Anthony Kenny, *Descartes: Philosophical Letters*, Minneapolis: University of Minnesota press, 1981: 50.

34. I am using this term to include: Kohlberg's moral dilemmas approach; the Canadian Critical Issues Series from O.I.S.E.; the Public Issues Series associated with Donald W. Oliver et al.; and the Humanities Curriculum Project associated with the Schools Council in England.

35. See Mary Anne Raywid, "Perspectives on the struggle against indoctrination," *Educational Forum 47*, 2, 1984: 137-54.

36. Lawrence Stenhouse, "The humanities curriculum project: the rationale," *Theory into Practice 10*, 3, 1971: 154-62.

37. Lawrence Kohlberg, *The Philosophy of Moral Development*, San Fransisco: Harper and Row, 1981: 27.

38. D. W. Oliver and M. J. Bane, "Moral education: is reasoning enough?" in C. M. Beck et al. (eds.), *Moral Education: Interdisciplinary Approaches*, Toronto: University of Toronto Press, 1971: 257.

39. See Kohlberg, *The Philosophy of Moral Development*, op. cit.: 12.

40. See Stenhouse, "The humanities curriculum project," op. cit.: 156.

41. Kohlberg, op. cit.: 27. For some of the complexities involved in specifying what open-minded teaching would involve, see chapter 3 of this collection.

42. See Peter Geach, "Plato's Euthyphro," *The Monist 50*, 1966: 369-82.

43. Kohlberg, op. cit.: 9.

44. Contrast the enormous literature in philosophy of education on the topic of indoctrination with the very limited discussion of open-mindedness.

5

Open-mindedness in the Education of Young Children

It is commonly thought, even by those who are sympathetic towards open-mindedness as an aim of education at the higher levels, that young children are not ready for an approach to teaching and learning which emphasizes this attitude. This chapter takes issue with this popular view.

Russell and Dewey

Many teachers and parents are hesitant about endorsing open-mindedness as an aim of elementary education. It is worth noting, therefore, that John Dewey and Bertrand Russell, the two great philosophers of education whose ideas helped to shape the modern elementary school, had no such hesitation. Russell's book *On Education*[1] is, of course, subtitled *Especially in early childhood* and contains the ringing declaration that open-mindedness should be one of the qualities that education aims at producing. Russell makes it clear that he has not momentarily overlooked the fact that he is supposedly writing about the education of young children by going out of his way to argue that open-mindedness is *especially* important in youth. The telling point he makes in this connection is simply that the exigencies of practical life will effectively close off many options later on as choices we have to make narrow the range of choices realistically available to us.

Like Russell, John Dewey gives a prominent place to open-mindedness in his account of those attitudes which are vital in education;[2] and Dewey is keenly aware that attitudes tend to run a poor third to knowledge and skills when the aims of education are discussed. Dewey calls our attention to what he labels the greatest of all pedagogical fallacies, namely the idea that the student is only learning the particular item of knowledge or skill he or she is studying at the time.[3] The moral is clear. If teachers fail to present an example of open-mindedness in their work, this will very likely rub off on the students who will cling to familiar ideas.

These are important, practical considerations, but there is good reason to suppose that philosophical confusion interferes with ready assent to them. One persistent confusion about open-mindedness is that it leads to, or is even the same as, scepticism. It seems enormously difficult to keep these two, very different ideas distinct. Even sophisticated thinkers have been known to slip up. Isaiah Berlin, in a television interview with Bryan Magee, shifts imperceptibly from talk of curiosity and critical scrutiny (which do have to do with open-mindedness) to talk of scepticism.[4] Similarly, David Suzuki advocates scepticism when it is clear *in context* that the idea he has in mind is open-mindedness.[5] These slips, however, may encourage conceptual confusion.

If parents and teachers are opposed to scepticism, that is admirable. There is no merit in doubting something in the absence of any grounds for doubt. It is no mark of an educated outlook to have a great number of doubts if these exist without a rational basis. Teachers are surely right to be unhappy if their young students "argue every point" regardless of whether or not they have a serious objection. Bertrand Russell wanted to know why incredulity should be thought of as any better than credulity, and the question is a good one. It is not scepticism which science should foster but rather what Russell called a kind of half-way house between scepticism and dogmatism, and this ground is occupied by open-mindedness. We are willing to believe, but not blindly like dogmatists; and we are willing to listen to doubts without giving up on belief in the manner of sceptics. But the temptation to view scepticism and dogmatism as exhausting the options seems almost overwhelming.

Questioning by students can be taken to excess and can interfere with other learning. This is not a reason, however, to abandon open-mindedness but rather points up the need to strike a balance here as elsewhere. We want our students to become interested in reading books, but not presumably at the expense of working on math problems. We do not, I think, refuse to teach children to tell the truth because telling the truth can be taken to excess. And if children are ever to sort out the point where a useful rule breaks down, or a good habit goes too far, open-mindedness is the very thing they will need.

The second great source of confusion and concern is the idea that open-mindedness means being ready to believe anything, hence parents fear that if the attitude is promoted their children will begin to adopt all manner of outrageous beliefs or, worse, engage in objectionable behavior. This confusion means, unfortunately, that Dewey's famous distinction has not been appreciated, though a clearer statement of it could hardly be imagined. Open-mindedness, Dewey insisted, is not the same as empty-mindedness.[6] The open-minded person is not someone ready to accept any idea which comes along, but someone prepared to consider what is to be said for and against an idea. It does not mean actually changing your mind every time the slightest objection is raised against any of your beliefs. If it did mean these things, it would indeed foster that very mindlessness which contemporary critics have ascribed to our schools.

To be open-minded, by contrast, is to be willing to have one's views influenced by evidence and reason. It is all too easy to become so comfortable with our convictions that we refuse to reconsider them, or even fail to see that they can be questioned at all. But this is not to say that open-mindedness encourages fence-sitting or is inconsistent with having convictions. It is how a person reacts to objections to his or her convictions which gives us a clue to that person's open-mindedness or the lack of it, not the having of convictions itself. A source of confusion here is the fact that the expression "keeping an open mind" is used when we have not made up our minds. When we have made up our minds, however, there is no reason why we cannot remain open-minded individuals capable of revising that conviction if that is warranted.

Learning how to learn would remain little more than a slogan if open-mindedness were not pursued. Elementary teachers have appreciated the need for students to learn how to go on learning on their own, to learn how to inquire. There may be general skills which can be taught to help the student become an independent learner, but these skills need to be combined with attitudes which make on-going learning attractive. One of the most important lessons we have to learn is a willingness to let new experiences sink in, to avoid roadblocks thrown up by prejudice.

From one point of view, the question about the need for elementary teachers to be open-minded is otiose. We do, after all, want our children to have teachers in school who are, first and foremost, educated persons; and the idea of an educated yet closed-minded individual is a contradiction in terms. This short way of dealing with the problem, important as it is in establishing a limit, will not quite do, however, since even open-minded teachers can place more or less emphasis on the attitude. One reason for teachers to make it an *important* aspect of their overall approach is simply that our earliest teachers have considerable influence on our subsequent development, or so longitudinal studies would suggest.

Recent Doubts

Some philosophers have argued that education is not a continuous process from early schooling to graduate school, that it refers to two quite distinct processes, socialization and individuation.[7] Thus, Richard Rorty argues that "it is not, and never will be, the function of lower-level education to challenge the prevailing concensus about what is true."[8] In short, for Rorty, the proper business of elementary and secondary education is socialization, making students culturally literate, familiarizing the young with what their elders take to be true. If this job were done properly, then the colleges and universities could give up the remedial work which present circumstances force upon them and concentrate on their distinctive role of generating doubt, firing the imagination, and promoting critical thought.[9]

One can agree with Rorty that society rightly expects that the elementary and secondary schools will teach what is generally held to be true. The first objection to his proposed dichotomy, however, is that the task of teaching what is generally believed is not incompatible with fostering a sense of alternative possibilities. To learn that such and such is generally believed to be the case does not preclude developing at the same time a realization that something else might turn out to be the case. Rorty asserts that socialization has to come *before* individuation, but does not explain why they cannot occur *pari passu*. One reason why they should go hand in hand is Dewey's point that "everything the teacher does, as well as the manner in which he does it, incites the child to respond in some way or other, and each response tends to set the child's attitude in some way or other."[10] Rorty claims to be a fairly faithful follower of Dewey in his views, but it seems to me that he might well be charged with committing "the greatest of all pedagogical fallacies."[11]

Certainly, Rorty is right to reject that caricature of Dewey which still turns up and portrays Dewey as peddling what Rorty calls nondirective nonsense. Dewey, indeed, is a great champion of information in the process of education and was fond of reminding us that thinking cannot go on in a vacuum. Nevertheless, Dewey was well aware that "amassing information always tends to escape from the ideal of wisdom or good judgment" and quite explicitly points out the danger of thinking that scholarship must come first: "The real desideratum is getting command of scholarship – or skill – under conditions that *at the same time* exercise thought."[12]

Open-mindedness is not to be achieved in an all-or-nothing manner. Experience suggests that even those who are relatively open-minded fall victim readily enough to bias and prejudice and fail to consider new ideas seriously. As an ideal, something which we cannot expect ever to realize in a full sense, it is an objective to be worked at from day to day, and there is much to be said for an early start. The value of an ideal is partly measured by those side benefits which come with it, and in the case of open-mindedness a gain in tolerance can be anticipated. This is because we cannot seriously claim to be open-minded with respect to new ideas if we will not permit their free expression. The circumstances which made it necessary for the Province of Alberta to establish a Committee on Tolerance and Understanding in 1983 also argue for the need for open-mindedness.[13]

These circumstances included not only the expression by a teacher of blatantly racist remarks, but also a systematic attempt to indoctrinate students. Although Keegstra was dealing with high school students, a study of the case reveals, as we shall see, that many of his students were incapable of open-minded thinking and some, by the greatest irony, even had the idea that Keegstra was an exemplar of the open-minded approach! The moral is that open-minded teaching cannot begin too soon if students are to protect themselves against indoctrination, or to recognize closed-mindedness when they meet it. There is obviously a warning in all of this for parents who are reluctant to allow their own children to think for themselves. If Dewey is right in his comment about the greatest of all pedagogical fallacies, our children may be learning *from us* to accept uncritically what the Keegstras have to offer.[14]

The temptation will surely be in practice to encourage open-mindedness in the teaching of school subjects, except where they start to encroach on matters too close to home for comfort such as community norms, religious beliefs and principles and the like. The hope will be to make certain topics *exempt* from the attitude. There is good reason, however, to think that this strategy cannot succeed. Once we encourage the attitude, as we must if indoctrination is to be countered, there can be no *arbitrary* limits placed on critical reflection. Open-mindedness is precisely the sort of attitude which seeks to challenge the arbitrary move. None of this is to say that open-mindedness prevents parents or teachers from trying to defend values, traditions, and habits they believe important. It only limits the way in which they can do this.

One benefit of teachers taking open-mindedness seriously and trying to foster this attitude in young students is that we might discourage what Jerry Popp has called the "pedagogical fallacy."[15] Teachers make the mistake of thinking that they have to jump in and set the children straight, and Popp identifies the mistake as that of seeing the children as adults with relatively settled views rather than as children whose views are likely to develop and change: "What we can do for them is not to judge what they do and say as if it were their final word on the subject, but to raise questions with them about it – to pursue it with them as far as they wish to go, and when they wish to stop, to think to ourselves: 'If this is really important it will come up again.'"[16] This attitude, however, presupposes that teachers believe in open-mindedness, and see the child engaged in a learning process in which much that is learned will be modified and revised as the child grows.

We cannot, unfortunately, assume that open-mindedness will take care of itself. A commentary in *Science* January 2, 1987 makes the frightening observation that the number one criterion for any school textbook is avoidance of controversy. History is rewritten, science distorted, and literature banned, and all in the name of open-mindedness. This kind of accommodation to the loudest voice is exactly what Dewey meant by empty-mindedness. Times are certainly bad when 72 Nobel Prize winners feel impelled to submit a brief to the United States Supreme Court in defence of open-minded science teaching in American schools. What can the individual teacher do in the face of such widespread opposition to the ideal? Here we may allow Russell the last word. You can always do *something*.[17]

Notes

1. Bertrand Russell, *On Education,* London: George Allen and Unwin, 1926.

2. John Dewey, *Democracy and Education,* New York: The Free Press, 1966 (Originally published, 1916). Also John Dewey, *How We Think* 2nd. ed., in Jo Ann Boydston (ed.), *John Dewey, The Later Works, 1925-53,* Vol. 8, Carbondale: Southern Illinois University Press, 1986 (Originally published, 1933).

3. John Dewey, *Experience and Education,* New York: Collier Books, 1963: 48 (Originally published, 1938).

4. Bryan Magee, *Men of Ideas,* Oxford: Oxford University Press, 1978: 2-3.

5. David Suzuki, "Science and society," in *The Canadian Encyclopaedia* (1985) Vol. 3: 1655-58.

6. John Dewey, *How We Think*, in Boydston (ed.), *John Dewey, The Later Works*, Vol. 8, op. cit.: 136

7. Richard Rorty, "Education without dogma," *Dissent 36*, 2, 1989: 198-204.

8. Rorty, op. cit.: 200.

9. Rorty, op. cit.: 200. In a subsequent paper, Rorty comments that, with luck, many students will go on to higher education. But many do not, and these do not have the same opportunity to develop critical ability. See Rorty, "The danger of over-philosophication: Reply to Arcilla and Nicholson," *Educational Theory 40*, 1, 1990: 41-44.

10. Dewey, *How We Think*, op. cit.: 159. Cf. also fn. 3 above.

11. I am not convinced that Dewey would have accepted the dichotomy suggested by Rorty. Dewey, for example, resisted the division between teaching and research: "The attempt to make a fixed line of demarcation between colleges that are simply teaching institutions and those that make a point of research is not, however, justified." Dewey, "Academic freedom," in Jo Ann Boydston (ed.), *John Dewey: The Middle Works, 1899-1924* Volume 6: 1910-1911: 460-4. In another context, Dewey spoke of "reactionaries that will claim that the main, if not the sole business of education is transmission of the cultural heritage." See *Experience and Education*, op. cit.: 78. Russell, incidentally, advocated breaking down the sharp division between school and university, urging that attitudes which are common in the university context be anticipated as early as possible in the schools. See his "Education for democracy," op. cit.: 533.

12. Dewey, *How We Think*, op. cit.: 163.

13. See Committee on Tolerance and Understanding, *Final Report*, Edmonton, 1984. A detailed examination of the Keegstra case, which prompted the formation of the committee, follows in the next chapter.

14. See further, chapter six.

15. Jerome A. Popp, "Teaching the ways of inquiry," *Illinois Schools Journal 57*, 3, 1977: 54-9. I think of this as the "last chance" fallacy.

16. op. cit.: 58.

17. Bertrand Russell, "On keeping a wide horizon," in *Russell 33-34*, 1979: 5-11 (Originally published, 1941).

6

Limiting The Freedom Of Expression
The Keegstra Case

The Keegstra case raises a dilemma for liberals who favor freedom of expression. Keegstra cannot, however, appeal to the "honest heretic" defence nor to a conception of the "marketplace of ideas." Keegstra's error has been wrongly diagnosed as seeking to convince. But this reaction neglects the spirit in which teaching is conducted and also the students' potential for critical reflection. The Keegstra case shows that philosophers of education have underestimated the threat posed by a sincere but misguided teacher. Classroom discussions of "theories" of the sort to which Keegstra subscribes need limits.

Memories are short, and soon a reference to Jim Keegstra, or an allusion to the Keegstra affair, will no doubt call for an explanatory footnote.[1] But in 1983-5, at the height of media attention in Canada, it seemed that an eponymous synonym for bigotry was about to enter the language. The Keegstra affair came almost overnight[2] to be seen as a paradigm case of indoctrination. There was general revulsion as the truth emerged, but we should follow Socrates in demanding more than a clear example. This was a case of miseducation, and we must be on guard against a number of potential misinterpretations. The idea of open-minded education excludes the possibility of viewing Keegstra as an "honest heretic" championing unpopular ideas in a free market.[3]

The General Background

Jim Keegstra believes in an international Jewish conspiracy to establish a world government, and regards the infamous *Protocols of the Learned Elders of Zion* as authentic. The fact that every reputable historian thinks this document a hoax is further proof for him that the conspiracy is alive and well. Keegstra's belief was central in his interpretation of historical events, and permeated his teaching throughout the year. In dealing with the Second World War, Keegstra taught that Zionists invented the Holocaust to attract supporters for their cause. When challenged by the authorities, Keegstra did not deny what he had been teaching, but sought to show that it was correct. His views were not smuggled in in the course of dealing with other issues. The Jewish conspiracy thesis *dominated* Keegstra's lessons and he remains eager to defend it. His willingness springs from a profound conviction that he possesses a truth which must be communicated to others who have been duped.

Keegstra's perverse historical views were such, and presented in such a way, that his teaching displayed and fostered anti-Semitic attitudes. When students made disparaging remarks about Jews in their essays, Keegstra added marginal comments to reinforce these ideas. The conspiracy allegation, combined with other dreadful fictions about Jews, led students to write about Jews as thugs, rapists, and assassins. Essays often argued that it was necessary to rid the world of dangerous Jews.

Disclosures of these teaching practices shocked Canadian society, and prompted the Province of Alberta to set up a Committee on Tolerance and Understanding in June 1983 which presented its final report in December 1984. The chairperson of the Committee remarked optimistically that "shocking revelations can become the catalyst from which flow a myriad of positive responses."[4] If teachers are not to shun controversy, however, a number of confused responses to the case need to be considered.

Villains are sometimes portrayed as martyrs. One hears mutterings about the value of open-mindedness, and the suggestion that Keegstra championed free inquiry. Many close to the scene were confused about the application of fundamental principles. Most Canadians now think that justice was done in dismissing Keegstra from the teaching profession, but since a revisionist thesis might be advanced, we need a clear grasp of the reasons which warranted termination of his contract and expulsion from the profession.

Buttons proclaiming "Freedom of Speech" were very much in evidence at the various judicial proceedings which began in 1984. Keegstra's lawyer, Douglas Christie, reportedly declared the case would be "the greatest test of freedom of speech this country has ever seen."[5] The Alberta Teachers' Association representative assigned to assist Keegstra answer the various charges brought by the Board, also insisted Keegstra's freedom of speech in the classroom was being curtailed.[6] Canadian civil libertarians denounced the prosecution of Keegstra as censorship, though some agreed that he had abused his position as a teacher and was rightly dismissed.[7]

Some of Keegstra's former students continue to believe he was silenced because the authorities were not committed to open inquiry. One student is quoted as saying that "perhaps people are scared he's stumbled onto the truth, and they don't want to know about it." The winner of the school's highest graduating award remained a loyal supporter of Keegstra *and* his ideas: "I'm trying so hard to be open-minded and they're close-minded."[8] Keegstra insisted he had presented an alternative point of view to make his students think,[9] and claimed that he advised his students that the position he defended "was only a theory,"[10] and not widely accepted.

The charge of bias came up frequently. One commentator, however, in reviewing the allegation that the students were not offered well-articulated alternatives, adds the qualification that "the problem of biased teaching will arise with every teacher."[11] A student is quoted as saying he had abandoned the idea of a career in teaching because he might slip up, say something inappropriate, and land in jail.[12] The idea lurking behind both of these reactions is that bias is inevitable.

Keegstra was widely regarded by students, colleagues, and the Alberta Teachers' Association as a good teacher. The principal at the time of Keegstra's dismissal testified that Keegstra did "a very thorough job" of classroom preparation, and that he had never heard Keegstra "call down another group except maybe Communists or Zionists."[13] A former principal commented that Keegstra's first qualification as a teacher was his "command of discipline."[14] Keegstra's classroom management skills have earned near universal praise. The Superintendent who pursued the case against Keegstra said that the issue was not Keegstra's competence as a teacher or his ability to teach the subject matter.[15]

There is enough confusion in these various reactions to warrant a careful examination of the assumptions which they reveal. We shall see that some who have shed light on this affair have also added to the confusion. Furthermore, there are ideas in circulation, advanced by philosophers who may never have heard of this case, which come to grief in the light of this sorry episode.

An Honest Heretic?

A liberal in the tradition of John Stuart Mill will, I think, experience some tension in considering this case.

> If all mankind minus one were of one opinion, mankind would be no more justified in silencing that one person than he, if he had the power, would be justified in silencing mankind.[16]

Yet, effectively, Keegstra *was* silenced, since the revocation of his teaching license removed a necessary condition of his employment. Where, in the words of Justice Holmes, is that "free trade in ideas" which ought to characterize education? Have we abandoned the idea that "the best test of truth is the power of the thought to get itself accepted in the competition of the market?"

In some ways, moreover, Keegstra does resemble the honest heretic rather than the furtive conspirator. Sidney Hook's classic distinction revealed differences showing why the heretic must be tolerated and the conspirator suppressed. The liberal, Hook wrote, "stands ready to defend the honest heretic no matter what his views against any attempt to curb him."[17] Like the heretic, Keegstra did not shrink from publicity. In the words of one commentator, "furtiveness is alien to him."[18] Keegstra, as far as we know, was in the service of no organized movement, though he joined the Canadian League of Rights and obtained much of his material from this group. There is every reason to agree that Keegstra sees himself as a solitary soldier.[19] The telltale signs of conspiracy are not to be found and not because the tracks have been covered.

Although no conspirator, however, Keegstra is only in part an honest heretic. Concerning the frank admission of the *content* of his views, Keegstra *is* the honest, forthright individual generally portrayed.[20] Keegstra did not conceal what he had been teaching when cross-examined at the Board of Reference inquiry, and his claim to have been teaching the required curriculum was not a lie but a mistaken belief. When we consider Keegstra's *methodology,* however, the ascription of honesty becomes suspect. Keegstra did alert his students to the fact that his theories were not widely shared and may even have advised them of the importance of examining different points of view.[21] But the evidence overwhelmingly suggests that his practice violated these principles.

First, Justice McFadyen established that *none* of the sources to which Keegstra directed his students contained a different point of view on the theory of history he propounded.[22] It is inconceivable that Keegstra was unaware of any such. Second, when students ventured to draw on sources other than those Keegstra approved, either their work was not assessed at all or assessed adversely.[23] Keegstra believes that sources critical of his position have been censored to conceal the truth, but he owed his students an honest account of alternative views in terms which defenders might accept as full and fair.[24] Third, Keegstra *encouraged* sweeping generalizations by his students by making comments calculated to confirm or support such views.[25] This makes a mockery of Keegstra's claim to be fostering the ability to discriminate between alternatives.[26]

Keegstra fails to qualify as an honest heretic in the classroom and forfeits the protection otherwise due. Appeal to the notion of a marketplace of ideas collapses because Keegstra's classes were systematically biased to inculcate at every opportunity the Jewish conspiracy theory. The notes, topics, readings, written comments, attitudes, and a grading system which rewarded agreement, were part of a strategy intended to convince students that a certain view of history was true. The decisive point is that the ground was cut from under the feet of any opposition by making the theory *immune* to counter-evidence. Potential counter-evidence was taken as *further* evidence of the conspiracy portrayed as controlling the *sources* of evidence, namely textbooks, the media and so on. Conspiracies can occur, of course, and it is doctrinaire to dismiss such claims *a priori.* But we need evidence that one exists, and refutation must be possible in principle. In frustrating the falsification challenge,[27] Keegstra revealed the disingenuous character of his teaching.

These criticisms are consistent with support for that strong tradition in philosophy of education which encourages students to become involved in the critical examination of controversy. Passmore has pointed out the limitations of teaching for critical thinking when criticism is reserved for "those who do not fully adhere to the accepted beliefs."[28] Russell advocated "the most vehement and terrific argumentation on all sides of every question,"[29] and maintained that there must be no requirement that teachers express only majority opinions. Strong enthusiasms, Russell said, are perfectly appropriate.[30] In protecting his own one-sided view from criticism, however, Keegstra subverted the critical approach to teaching.

Unfortunately, some commentators have not questioned the plausibility of the marketplace defence used by Keegstra supporters. Consider the following suggestions:

The school is not a marketplace of ideas

Keegstra did not, however, attempt to foster a marketplace of ideas and it is misguided to suggest, as some have done, that this case shows the inappropriateness of the marketplace ideal in public schooling:

> The elementary and high-school systems are not viewed by civil libertarians as part of the public forum we seek to protect from censorship. We doubt it makes sense to apply a notion such as "censorship" when we judge the professional wisdom of what is chosen for the attention of not yet fully-fledged minds.[31]

The common assumption, exemplified here, is that academic freedom has application only in the university context.[32] But if an open forum for discussion is appropriate at *any* level, then progressively there must be an anticipation of the practice during earlier stages of education. A rigid division between different levels is arbitrary. The "not yet fully-fledged minds" include 18 year-old adults in grade XII, or equivalent, who will be university students within three months. We might label the error here the fallacy of the magic transition. Finally, there is no reason to conclude that the concept of censorship does not apply in the school context. When books are removed from the library and words deleted from textbooks to accommodate complaints, censorship certainly exists.

Teaching is not preaching

Anthony Blair distinguishes two uses of argument to illustrate what he sees as the defect in Keegstra's approach.[33] He distinguishes between (a) argument used to *convince* and (b) argument used to *inquire*, and Keegstra emerges as having attempted to convert the students to his position rather than as having shown them how to employ argument to test ideas. Keegstra's use of argument to convince, Blair claims, is very different from the attempt to foster open-mindedness.

First, however, notice the either/or nature of Blair's suggestion. The implication is that the teacher must opt for the second use of argument, that is to inquire, since argument used to convince "will often be perceived by those untutored in its deployment as an instrument of coercion."[34] Certainly, teachers who take a stand on some question and attempt to convince their students must *also* teach the use of argument as a tool of inquiry if the students are to have the wherewithal to assess the teacher's position critically. But the use of argument to convince is not in itself a violation of educational principles. What matters is how the argument is *conducted*. Keegstra's approach was a travesty of the Socratic ideal of following the argument where it leads, and for this he stands condemned. The obvious danger in Blair's diagnosis is that we are close to embracing teacher neutrality as an absolute principle.

Second, open-mindedness does not require neutrality. Blair glosses open-mindedness as "withholding judgment until one has thoroughly canvassed alternatives and seriously considered points of view other than one's own."[35] Though popular, this is inadequate as a general account. What matters is how one's convictions are held.[36] Here the central question is whether or not they are regarded as revisable in the light of emerging evidence and fresh argument. Keegstra is no champion of open-mindedness not because he held, and defended, certain convictions, but because these were *not* revisable; they had been granted immunity. Teaching is not preaching, but this is consistent with teachers employing argument in the attempt to convince.

Keegstra's student who claims to be open-minded is typical of those John Dewey criticized,[37] who naively think open-mindedness is indicated by merely adopting, or flirting with, unconventional ideas. Ironically, this student has been *prevented* from rationally reviewing his beliefs by coming to think all contrary evidence is untrustworthy. Moreover, the student has been discouraged from developing the capacity to recognize that his position comes with a spurious guarantee of its own certainty.

Despite endless debate over the analysis of indoctrination, it is reassuring that the parent responsible for initiating the complaint that eventually led to decisive action against Keegstra closed her letter to the Superintendent with the words: "As our children are being sent to school for education, not indoctrination, I appeal to you to dismiss Mr. Keegstra from teaching those classes in which our children will be enrolled."[38] This is the apposite distinction because the students were adopting beliefs in such a way that rational criticisms were defused. Many professionals were not able to articulate or even recognize the distinction in question. Some students did *eventually* start to question what they had come to believe following certain extraordinary steps including, for some, a trip to Dachau (even these measures were not uniformly successful.) The crucial point is not that the students' beliefs could never be dislodged, but that a *pattern* of thinking had emerged inimical to evidence and argument.[39]

Allen Pearson fears that certain presuppositions in the teaching context helped bring about the undesirable consequence of closed-minded allegiance to irrational beliefs.[40] The logic of the teaching situation, he argues, is that any teacher must be considered rational otherwise there would be no point attending to him or her: "One cannot be a learner if one does not accept that the teacher is acting rationally."[41] Teachers like Keegstra, Pearson adds, have difficulty with cynical or very sceptical students, but these are hardly desirable traits.

Pearson's pessimism is, I think, premature. Cynicism and skepticism are *not* the only defences against an irrational teacher. Inexplicably, Pearson fails to mention *critical reflection.* If schools developed critical ability in students, and discouraged deferential acceptance, learners would not be so vulnerable. There is an unavoidable criticism here of the teachers who taught these students before Keegstra. Few philosophers have noted that students need to be trained to resist indoctrination.[42] Keegstra's skill shows how important such an ability is, for Keegstra was unable to recognize his own teaching as indoctrination. The psychology of the classroom is often such that uncritical acquiescence results,[43] but there is no *logical* barrier to success as Pearson implies. One can learn from teachers even if one fails to agree with their ideas, or suspects that the ideas presented are spurious. One can *understand* what the beliefs are and why some people hold them, and resolve to assess their merits. Typically, we presume that the teacher believes what he or she is saying, but we need not, and must not, assume that the claims are true. Pearson overlooks provisional agreement where we accept "for the sake of argument" but reserve the right to subject the beliefs in question to later critical examination. If these attitudes sound sophisticated, the Keegstra case nevertheless indicates their necessity. We expect we can learn something valuable from our teachers, but expectations are not always fulfilled.

The Principle of Tolerance

The Province of Alberta moved soon after the Keegstra revelations to establish a Committee on Tolerance and Understanding. Its interim report maintained that a basic aim of education is to instil in children an appreciation of our democratic traditions, characterized by an attitude of tolerance, understanding, and respect for others, *no matter what their origins or values may be.*[44] The final report, however, omitted these concluding words. It likely occurred to someone that the deleted statement made no sense in the light of the circumstances which gave rise to the Committee's work. Were tolerance required no matter what a person's values, then Keegstra's intolerance would itself have to be tolerated.

Certainly some took that quixotic course. The Alberta Teachers' Association representative who defended Keegstra at the early hearings said he could accept different points of view being a fairly tolerant person. He maintained that Keegstra had advanced a different point of view as was his right.[45] This comment exemplifies the confusion mentioned earlier that leads some to see Keegstra as a champion of free inquiry silenced by an intolerant society.[46] Keegstra's right to *mention* and *discuss* alternative points of view and interpretations had never been challenged by the School Board, though it had given directions about balance. In his first letter to Keegstra, Superintendent David wrote he had not intended to muzzle Keegstra's academic freedom nor to limit his intellectual integrity. Controversial interpretations were not to be suppressed but all positions were to be presented in as unbiased a way as possible.[47]

Appealing uncritically to the principle of tolerance, the Alberta Teachers' Association in effect extended tolerance to indoctrination.

The wording on bias avoids the naive position that a bias-free presentation is possible without suggesting that the amount and nature of bias is quite beyond our control. The problem of biased teaching may arise with every teacher, but not in the same way nor to the same degree. Although teachers can slip into bias, tolerance here is appropriate when teachers display a willingness to review their performances and the judgments of others critically. Keegstra sincerely believed his own position was correct, but he could and should have been aware that he was not presenting other views impartially. If we tolerate the systematic distortion of issues in teaching, we cannot claim to have a serious concern for our students' education.

The Keegstra case is useful in philosophy of education as a touchstone for testing philosophical generalizations.[48] If we have confidence in a particular judgment, we can ask how a certain general principle fares when viewed in the light of that judgment. Mary Warnock argues that a teacher is not invariably required to remain neutral on controversial issues.[49] It would be a pity if confusion resulting from the Keegstra case gave undeserved support to the neutral teacher movement. Russell saw clearly that a teacher could display strong enthusiasms but there remained an obligation to give an impartial account of what really happened. Mary Warnock, however, exaggerates the benefits of non-neutrality risking undue teacher influence on students. She maintains there is only benefit in the contemplation of someone who has principles: "The first rule of teaching is sincerity, even if one's sincerity is dotty or eccentric." Concerning the danger of winning over students too easily, she assures us that time will remedy this, if remedy is needed.[50] Mary Warnock was not commenting on Keegstra, but how do her comments stand up in the light of this case?

A number of points should be made. First, it is clear we cannot say that Keegstra has no principles. He does not have, as Mackie once put it, a new principle for every case.[51] Keegstra has his own principles and will not abandon them for convenience or advantage. But although we may admire his courage and sincerity, it is not true that there is *nothing but benefit* in contemplating his actions. His principles are flawed from an educational perspective. Keegstra's concern for truth, which he often stressed, amounted to an all-consuming desire that his students believe what he accepted as true. In Russell's language, the will to believe overshadowed the wish to find out.[52] This desire was not tempered by a concern to help students weigh evidence and formulate independent judgments. The clearest evidence of Keegstra's position and his blind attachment to it is his lack of concern over the appalling ignorance and illiteracy displayed in student essays.[53]

Second, in characterizing perverse sincerity as eccentric or dotty, Mary Warnock has overlooked more serious harms. We smile at eccentricity or dottiness, but these friendly descriptions hardly capture Keegstra's mind-set. Having students think of Jews as "gutter rats" cannot be airily dismissed as eccentricity. When a student writes that we must get rid of every Jew in existence, we have gone beyond the dotty. The case shows a failure of imagination on Mary Warnock's part with respect to the forms perversity can take. Furthermore, this case makes one less sanguine about time effecting a remedy. Bercuson and Wertheimer fear that Keegstra's students may become the bearers of medieval myths in the future.[54] Interviews with some students two years after Keegstra's dismissal provide little basis for sharing Mary Warnock's confidence, yet much more than the mere passage of time was at work in this case.[55] Mary Warnock had not envisaged a case where the beliefs acquired immunized one against counter-evidence, so that the passage of time would make no difference or even make matters worse.

We should be reluctant to embrace the level of tolerance suggested by Mary Warnock's comment. Should we even tolerate the *inclusion* of ideas such as the Jewish conspiracy theory? Many will find the theory offensive and it is widely regarded as totally implausible. There is, however, a powerful tradition in philosophy of education which supports the inclusion of controversial material and open discussion of related issues. But it is doubtful that the Jewish conspiracy theory properly counts as a controversial historical thesis. Reputable historians do not seriously debate it. A few dispute the opinion held by experts but have not succeeded in making the matter controversial. From the perspective of historical research, the theory is a non-starter.

Should it also be ignored in teaching? Surely, the school might give the theory unwitting support by deeming it worthy of mention. Its exclusion, however, might fuel the suspicion that the theory has some credibility, a suspicion actually voiced by some students.[56] If suppression of such a view could be effectively carried out in society as a whole, this danger would disappear, but that is not a realistic possibility quite apart from considerations of moral acceptability. Given this dilemma, a compromise might be proposed, namely to ignore the theory unless it is brought up by a student. This strategy, however, presupposes that students genuinely feel comfortable raising issues, otherwise they might be privately nursing their suspicions. We need to remember here that students raise few questions of any kind in class.[57]

The traditional response to the dilemma invokes the ideal that truth should emerge in open discussion. There is no need to exclude the theory since its absurdity can be demonstrated. We can explain that it is included not because it is important, interesting, or plausible, but simply because students may encounter it. Recently, however, Schauer has cast doubt on the so-called argument from truth:

> The argument from truth is very much a child of the Enlightenment, and of the optimistic view of the rationality and perfectibility of humanity it embodied. . . . People are not nearly so rational as

the Enlightenment assumed, and without this assumption the empirical support for the argument from truth evaporates.[58]

Schauer reminds us that truth has no inherent ability to gain general acceptance. The argument from truth leads to the dubious assumption that the search for truth is the supreme value.

It is not evident, however, that these points carry weight in the context of education. In tolerating open discussion of reprehensible views, the assumption is not that students are thoroughly rational. Rather, one of the central aims of education is to *further* their development as rational agents. To curtail discussion in schools because people are not always rational would deprive students of the very practice that might lead to the development of rational abilities. If it is true now that people are not particularly good at distinguishing truth from falsity, it is especially important for schools to look for ways in which this ability can be developed. Particular considerations might outweigh the importance of open discussion of certain issues at certain times, but present abilities are not the determining factor. Schauer says that we must take the public as it is, but in the context of education our sights must be on what the students *can be*. The study of bad arguments is an important part of learning to argue effectively. Prior practice in this area would have served Keegstra's students well.

If we tolerate the discussion of such a theory, should we also tolerate the teacher indicating support for it? Keegstra's own approach was obviously unacceptable, and we might note Russell's point that when the experts agree, the opposite opinion cannot be regarded as certain. This alone would condemn Keegstra's teaching as profoundly misleading.[59] What, however, of the teacher who avoids that error, presents all views fully and fairly, but reveals a personal inclination to accept a theory universally discredited and offensive.

Let us distinguish this case from two others. Consider, first, the fact that various groups find aspects of the school curriculum offensive. An example might be a reference to atrocities carried out in the past. Here, it is vital to ask if the atrocities are indeed part of the historical record. If so, we would distort historical inquiry were we to allow our preferences to dictate what enters our history books or lessons. There is a positive obligation to be faithful to the discipline and report what happened. There is also a moral obligation to try to ensure that such facts do not lead to prejudice against those associated with the country in question.

Consider, secondly, the debate over creation science. This position is utterly discredited, but it is not in itself morally offensive whatever one may think of the tactics sometimes employed in its defence. One simply reveals naiveté in subscribing to such views. If a teacher reveals sympathy for creation science, appeal to eccentricity will suffice to justify tolerance if the teacher at the same time manages to present orthodox science as it would be presented by a teacher who personally regarded it as serious.

The Jewish conspiracy theory, however, is both discredited and offensive. A teacher who reveals that he or she accepts it necessarily alienates all those students, not only Jews, who take offence at others being falsely accused of general wickedness. In ordinary life, we can usually avoid those who utter offensive remarks, but reasonable avoidability does not exist at school.[60] Students are obliged to attend and not normally permitted to choose which section of a course they will take, and therefore which teacher they will have, when multiple sections are available.[61] I conclude that in such cases the expression of the teacher's private sympathies should not be permitted.

Concluding Comment

Recall that Keegstra was widely hailed as a "good teacher." This suggests the dispiriting conclusion that this appraisal has lost its essential meaning. The judgment was based on the fact that Keegstra maintained discipline, and was totally unrelated to any consideration of the knowledge, skills, and attitudes being learned by his students. Possibly this case will lead us to think out more carefully what a good teacher does. In doing this, we will be stimulated, I think, by an observation from Russell that might have applied to this very case:

> Love of power is the chief danger of the educator, as of the politician; the man who can be trusted in education must care for his pupils on their own account, not merely as potential soldiers in an army of propagandists for a cause.[62]

Notes

1. It might read as follows. James Keegstra (b. 1934) taught in the province of Alberta from 1961 to 1983. Having qualified as an auto mechanic in 1957, he enrolled as a part-time student at what is now the University of Calgary, pursuing a B.Ed. program with a concentration in industrial arts. Before graduating in 1967, he taught industrial arts and other subjects, finally securing a permanent position at Eckville High School, Eckville, in 1968. He gradually came to teach classes in history and social studies, and it was his teaching here and his failure to conform to the prescribed curriculum which led to his dismissal from the school, effective January 1983. This decision was upheld by Justice Elizabeth McFayden in a Board of Reference ruling in April 1983. In October 1983, the Alberta Minister of Education revoked Keegstra's teaching license, and he was expelled from the Alberta Teachers' Association. In July 1985, Keegstra was convicted under section 281.2 of the Canadian Criminal Code of wilfully promoting hatred against the Jews, a charge arising directly from his classroom activities, and fined $5000.00. In June 1988, the conviction was overturned by the Alberta Court of Appeal on the grounds that the law in question violates the Canadian Charter of Rights and Freedoms. The Crown's appeal was heard in the Supreme Court of Canada in December 1989, and in December 1990 the Supreme Court of Canada ruled in a 4-3 judgment that the hate-promotion statute is constitutional. The case was sent back to the Alberta Court of Appeal where the original conviction was overturned in 1991 on a technicality.

In July 1992, following a new trial on the same charge, Keegstra was again found guilty and fined $3000.00.

2. Much of the credit for bringing the case to national attention must go to the documentary "Lessons in hate" shown on the CBC's *The Journal*, May 2, 1983.

3. The best general introduction to the case is: David Bercuson and Douglas Werthei-mer, *A Trust Betrayed: The Keegstra Affair*, Toronto: Doubleday Canada, 1985.

4. Committee on Tolerance and Understanding, *Final Report*, Edmonton, Alberta, 1984. Headed by Ron Ghitter, the committee came to be known as the Ghitter Committee.

5. *Macleans*, June 25, 1984: 29.

6. See Bercuson and Wertheimer, *A Trust Betrayed*, op. cit.: 106.

7. See John Dixon, "The politics of opinion," *The Canadian Forum 66*, April 1986: 7-10.

8. For the reactions of the students, see Robert Mason Lee, "Keegstra's children," *Saturday Night*, May 1985: 38-46.

9. See Bercuson and Wertheimer, *A Trust Betrayed*, op. cit.: 112.

10. This phrase is used in the report of the Board of Reference, presumably echoing Keegstra's testimony. See footnote 1 above.

11. Christopher Podmore, "Our freedoms of expression: reflections on the Zundel and Keegstra affairs," *Humanist in Canada 18*, 4, 1985-6: 16-17.

12. See Steve Mertl and John Ward, *Keegstra: The Issues, The Trial, The Conse-quences*, Saskatoon: Western Producer Prairie Books, 1985: 133.

13. Cited in Arthur M. Schwartz, "Teaching hatred: The politics and morality of Canada's Keegstra affair," *Canadian and International Education 15*, 2, 1986: 5-28. Apparently, abuse is acceptable if the targets are limited. Note the use of slang expressions by an educational leader at a formal hearing.

14. See Schwartz, "Teaching hatred," op. cit.: 13.

15. Letter from R. K. David to James Keegstra, March 9, 1982. Document 3 in the appendix to Bercuson and Wertheimer, *A Trust Betrayed*, op. cit.

16. John Stuart Mill, *On Liberty*, ch. 2.

17. Sidney Hook, "Heresy, yes - conspiracy, no," in Harry K. Girvetz (ed.), *Contem-porary Moral Issues*, Belmont: Wadsworth, 1963: 62-71. An extract from a book by Sidney Hook with the same title.

18. K. Mazurek, "Indictment of a profession: the continuing failure of professional accountability," *Teacher Education 32*, 1988: 58.

19. Bercuson and Wertheimer, *A Trust Betrayed*, op. cit.: 15.

20. Mazurek, "Indictment of a profession," op. cit.: 58.

21. Bercuson and Wertheimer, *A Trust Betrayed*, op. cit.: 50.

22. Appeal to Board of Reference, 1983, p. 19 of transcript.

23. Bercuson and Wertheimer, *A Trust Betrayed*, op. cit.: 61.

24. See Alan Montefiore (ed.), *Neutrality and Impartiality: The University and Political Commitment*, London: Cambridge University Press, 1975: 18.

25. Lee, "Keegstra's children," op. cit.: 38.

26. Letter from Keegstra to Superintendent David, March 18, 1982. See document 4 in the appendix to Bercuson and Wertheimer, *A Trust Betrayed*, op. cit.

27. Antony Flew, *Thinking About Thinking*, Glasgow: Fontana/Collins, 1975: 55.

28. John Passmore, "On teaching to be critical," in R. S. Peters (ed.), *The Concept of Education*, London: Routledge and Kegan Paul, 1967: 197.

29. Bertrand Russell, "Education for democracy," op cit.: 529.

30. Bertrand Russell and Dora Russell, *Prospects of Industrial Civilization*, New York: Century, 1923: 255.

31. John Dixon, "The politics of opinion," op. cit.: 7. At the time the article was published, John Dixon was President of the British Columbia Civil Liberties Association.

32. See, for example, Anthony O'Hear, "Academic freedom and the university," *Journal of Philosophy of Education 22*, 1, 1988: 13-21. This point does not imply that academic freedom and freedom of speech are equivalent notions.

33. J. Anthony Blair, "The Keegstra affair: A test case for critical thinking," *History and Social Science Teacher 21*, 3, 1986: 158-164.

34. Blair, op. cit.: 161-2.

35. Blair, op. cit.: 162.

36. See my *Open-mindedness and Education*, op cit.; and my *In Defence of Open-mindedness*, op cit.

37. A good example is in John Dewey, *Democracy and Education*, op. cit.: 175.

38. Letter from Susan Maddox to R. K. David, October 11, 1982. Document 6 in the appendix to Bercuson and Wertheimer, *A Trust Betrayed*, op. cit.

39. The testimony of the teacher who had the unwelcome task of succeeding Keegstra at Eckville High and of counteracting his efforts is clear. See *The Globe and Mail*, April 11, 1985: 1-2.

40. Allen T. Pearson, "Teaching and rationality: The case of Jim Keegstra," *Journal of Educational Thought 20*, 1, 1986: 1-7.

41. op. cit.: 5

42. An exception is Noam Chomsky. See his "Toward a humanistic conception of education," in Walter Feinberg and Henry Rosemount, Jr. (eds.), *Work, Technology, and Education*, Urbana: University of Illinois Press, 1975: 204-20.

43. See Jim MacKenzie, "Authority," *Journal of Philosophy of Education 22*, 1, 1988: 57-65.

44. A portion of the interim report was published in *Canadian School Executive 4*, 2, 1984: 34. Emphasis mine.

45. See Bercuson and Wertheimer, *A Trust Betrayed*, op. cit.: 117.

46. Unfortunately, Bercuson and Wertheimer inadvertently add to the confusion. In making it clear that Harrison, the ATA's representative, had not defended Keegstra's right to teach the Jewish conspiracy theory as a fact of history, they add (as a criticism of the short clip of a longer interview with Harrison shown on CBC television) the comment that the public perception was that Harrison had defended "Keegstra's right to teach his students about a Jewish conspiracy." But, of course, Harrison had defended this, and the School Board had never challenged it. The wording blurs the

very distinction needed between teaching as a fact and teaching about a claim. See *A Trust Betrayed*, op. cit.: 117-8.

47. Letter from R. K. David to Keegstra, December 18, 1981. See Document 1 in the appendix to Bercuson and Wertheimer, *A Trust Betrayed,* op. cit.

48. Compare Joel Feinberg, *Social Philosophy*, Englewood Cliffs, NJ: Prentice-Hall, 1973.

49. Mary Warnock, "The neutral teacher," reprinted in William Hare and John P. Portelli (eds.), *Philosophy of Education: Introductory Readings*, op cit.: 177-186.

50. Mary Warnock, "The neutral teacher," op. cit.: 185.

51. J. L. Mackie, *Ethics: Inventing Right and Wrong*, Harmondsworth: Penguin Books, 1977: 156.

52. See Bertrand Russell, "Free thought and official propaganda," in Russell, *The Will To Doubt,* New York: Philosophical Library, 1958: 23.

53. One such essay is reproduced as document 11 in Bercuson and Wertheimer, *A Trust Betrayed*, op. cit.

54. Bercuson and Wertheimer, *A Trust Betrayed*, op. cit.: 187.

55. See Lee, "Keegstra's children," op. cit.

56. See earlier fn. 8.

57. See J. T. Dillon, "The remedial status of student questioning," *Journal of Curriculum Studies 20*, 3, 1988: 197-210.

58. Frederick Schauer, *Free Speech: A Philosophical Enquiry,* Cambridge: Cambridge University Press, 1982: 26

59. Bertrand Russell, "On the value of scepticism," in *The Will To Doubt, op. cit.: 39.*

60. See Joel Feinberg, *Social Philosophy*, op. cit.

61. This practice, incidentally, reveals the near universal assumption that a student in school may not evaluate his or her teachers, an assumption which clearly increases the difficulty any student would face in challenging someone like Keegstra.

62. Bertrand Russell, *Power: A New Social Analysis,* London: George Allen and Unwin, 1938: 304.

7

Alleged Bias in Children's Books

The Guidelines published in the United States by the Council on Interracial Books for Children in 1980 appeal to criteria such as language, omission, and caricature to support the view that certain popular children's books are racist. It is argued here, with reference to the books in question, that the guidelines blur the distinction between what is said and what sort of judgment it constitutes. Next it is shown that the interventionist, didactic role demanded of the writer in these guidelines ignores the complexities of literature. Finally, it is maintained that such factors as mood, tone, and humor need to be weighed in assessing caricature. Such guidelines may foster a distorted view of literary criticism, and encourage a tendency to read in too much. The serious issue of racism is in danger of being trivialized, and moral education of turning into didacticism. The distinction between a guideline and a mechanical rule needs to be preserved, and more sophisticated guidelines are required.

Introduction

It is clear that we often come to realize that our writing or teaching has been biased despite our best intentions. Bias distorts the account presented, and unless there is some special reason which justifies its use in a given context, it must be out of place in education where truth and accuracy are central values. Of course, the study of biased views will often be important, but bias itself will be avoided. Hence a set of guidelines for detecting bias would be extremely useful, since we would at least have a checklist to refer to in reviewing our practice and our chances of recognizing unconscious bias would be improved. Various publishing companies have issued such guidelines in recent years, but I will concentrate here on the widely-known and influential set produced by the Council on Interracial Books for Children in 1980.[1]

These guidelines were explained and developed in the context of a discussion of several novels and stories for children, and deal with various forms of bias. I will deal only with the topic of racism, and will show that the guidelines are often seriously inadequate, and that particular judgments based on them are erroneous. Clearly, such a topic could take one into several areas, including philosophy, literary criticism, and educational theory. My main purpose is to follow the advice of the Council itself and examine the guidelines with a "critical, questioning mind."[2] Thus my approach will be broadly philosophical, only drawing on literary points where appropriate to buttress an interpretation.

Towards the end, I will comment on certain educational issues of relevance to the philosophy of education which arise. There is no attempt to question the motives of the Council. But as we have already noticed, well-intentioned accounts may slip into bias and this applies *a fortiori* to accounts of bias itself.

I take racism to include both the doctrine that it is appropriate or necessary to discriminate between people on the basis of their racial background, and attitudes and practices which support such doctrine.[3] The notion of support here covers conscious and deliberate policy but must also be broad enough to include those comments and actions which reveal the racism which we manage to hide from ourselves.[4] It must not, however, be so broad that it includes whatever an avowed racist can misrepresent to his or her own advantage. If the latter were the case, no comment or action would be safe from the charge, and the concept would become empty. The fact then that, for example, the findings of psychology and sociology can be misrepresented so as to give support to racism does not show that such research is itself racist. On the other hand, our comments and actions may be racist though we sincerely maintain that we are not. The Council's guidelines stipulate that racism involves necessarily the back-up of institutional power.[5] This does not seem to me to be a necessary feature of the concept, but my criticisms do not depend upon this disagreement.

Language

It is not difficult to identify overt and blatant instances of racist language, though even here, as we will see later, we cannot immediately condemn a book as racist because it contains obvious examples of racist language. But language can also embody racist doctrine, and serve to give it support, in more subtle and hidden ways. The guidelines quite properly advise the reader to be on the lookout for "loaded words," such as savage, primitive, and wily, which have offensive overtones.[6] If, however, we examine the way in which the authors of the guidelines employ this criterion, it is clear that it requires some refinement. We are told, for example, that: *"The Slave Dancer* by Paula Fox tried to show the horrors of slavery and the slave trade, but was nevertheless filled with its own racism. The slaves had no individuality, no spirit, no brains. They were compared at one point to 'scrambling rats'."[7]

That certainly sounds suspicious, and none too subtle, but consider the context in the novel. The young boy, Jessie, who has been kidnapped by slave traders, is resting one night while the ship is anchored off-shore: "At midnight, or thereabouts, I heard a sound as though a thousand rats were scrambling up the hull of *The Moonlight*. I sprang from my hammock, found myself alone in our quarters, and raced up the ladder to the deck."[8]

Clearly, there is a sense in which it is true that at one point in the story the slaves are compared to scrambling rats. But it is the noise made by the slaves as they scramble aboard which prompts the thought, not the character of the slaves nor indeed anything about their observed behavior at all. The reader knows that the slaves are being boarded, and the boy knows that they are to be boarded at some time, but when he makes the comparison he does not know what the noise is. He cannot, therefore, be making derogatory remarks about the slaves. We need here a distinction between what is said and what it constitutes, and the vague guideline blurs this. Certainly, what the Council claims is said in the book is said; but whether or not it constitutes a derogatory judgment depends on contextual circumstances. Such a comparison may also be the content of a poignant and frighting description. Even if the boy had known that the noise was being made by the slaves, the above distinction would be relevant.

In point of fact, the comparison serves an important function in the novel from a literary standpoint, and cannot, therefore, be condemned as a gratuitous and dangerous image. It constitutes a kind of foreshadowing since the slaves are to share the hold with the rats which infest the ship. We come to see how horribly appropriate the image is. This consideration helps us to see that the remark is not a slip into a loaded description which helps to perpetuate the view that blacks are helpless and less than human. On the contrary, it underlines the evil of a doctrine which can lead to blacks being treated in this way.[9]

That the guidelines neglect the importance of context becomes abundantly clear when we read the following: ". . . how many of us speak of a day of woe as 'a black day' without realizing that those words equate black with bad and thus help to perpetuate racism."[10]

Now it is certainly true that we do come to realize that certain terms are much more offensive and demeaning than had once been imagined, and we can appreciate why titles such as *Ten Little Niggers* need to be revised. The word "black," however, has been used throughout the history of poetry, in various languages, from Homer to Shakespeare, to capture the idea of evil: "For I have shown thee fair, and thought thee bright, Who art as black as hell, as dark as night."[11]

There is no reason to believe that Shakespeare's imagery here subordinates people because of their color. It is surely possible to appreciate that when "black" is used figuratively to represent evil or woe, nothing derogatory is being said about blacks because nothing is being said about blacks at all. It would be equally mistaken to think that *Black Beauty* had an anti-racist message. These points might be omitted entirely were it not for the fact that allegations of racism of this sort seem likely to trivialize what is a serious moral issue.

The racist interpretation of ordinary language uses of the word "black" is quite implausible. First, the same language contains many uses of "white" where the connotation is unfavorable. We run up the white flag when we are forced to surrender. An issue is white-washed and something is made to seem better than it is. When we are cowardly we are said to be white-livered, and white-hot when in a state of extreme excitement. It seems unlikely that language users would build in racist remarks about themselves. Secondly, it is not difficult to identify alternative explanations for such expressions. White-wash has its origins in painting not racism, and white-livered rests on misconceptions in biology. When the sky is black or dark, bad weather is predictable and it is easy to see how this idea could be transferred to that of evil more generally.

Omission

The Council reminds us that racism by omission is possible and suggests that we consider this danger seriously now that minority groups are routinely represented in story books. For example: "A racist act may be presented but the author neglects to comment on it – which serves as implicit sanction of the act, leaving the younger reader with the impression that it was correct."[12]

We may wonder, however, if it is desirable, from a literary point of view, for the author to intervene with his or her own views about what is correct. Aristotle made the point in the *Poetics* that: "Homer deserves to be commended on many grounds, but mainly because he alone among the poets knew what his own role should be. The poet himself ought to say very little . . ."[13]

It will often strike us as pedantic, boring, and preachy for the author to tell us how to react. In this comment, the Council neglects its own sound advice that it is the final product which counts, not the intent.[14] In the guidelines, the author's intention and role has been over-emphasized at the expense of the effect and achievement. It is a simple mistake to think the views of the author are to be identified with those of the main, or any, character in the book, a mistake which is likely to be encouraged by the further recommendation that we delve into the author's biography and background. It is the work which is to be assessed, and we begin with a prejudice if we believe that a story must be racist because it was written by a certain person.

If the young reader is gaining the impression that the book sanctions racism because an act of racism is not explicitly condemned, there is something seriously wrong with the way in which he or she is being introduced to literature. It will perhaps be pointed out that we are speaking of books for children, and that the distinction between intention and achievement is too sophisticated in this context. On this point, however, I find myself in agreement with the Council when it remarks that: "the intellectual curiosity of an eleven or twelve-year-old deserves respectful challenges rather than mushy pablum."[15]

What is objectionable about *Bright April* by Marguerite de Angeli (Double-day, 1946) is that it is so crudely didactic. Be nice to those who are unfriendly, and in time they will come to like you. It might be objected here that racist views could be countered in the text without the overt intrusion of the author, thus avoiding a moralistic approach. Referring again to *The Slave Dancer*, the point is made that: "The book's main characters express hatred and disgust towards Blacks; there was no contradiction of their attitudes; so those were the emotions that received validity."[16]

It is not clear, however, why it would be inappropriate to say that the racist attitudes were left exposed in all their ugliness. The book's achievement is to depict racism in stark detail, a legitimate and important task, and one which is not racist at all. The effect is not to glorify racism, but to portray it vividly and honestly. The main character, Jessie, does not express hatred and disgust, and he is the character presented most sympathetically. The book also manages to avoid any kind of simplistic moral such as the triumph of good over evil. It is true that the black boy escapes to the North, but to what future we are not told. Unfortunately, the guidelines seem to suggest that stories necessarily contain a moral of some sort, but this is to encourage an immature approach to the study of literature.[17]

Racism by omission is also alleged in certain stories which are said to ignore the black person's perspective:

> "The white child learns to accept the Black as 'just like me'. *The Cay* by Theodore Taylor, which won a host of 'brotherhood' awards is a classic example of this . . . But what about a Black person's acceptance of the white. That is just automatically assumed."[18]

There are several problems with this. First, if the Council is correct in claiming that racism in the United States is white, it is natural that writers who deal with the problem of overcoming racism would want to illustrate the changing perspective of the white person who is racist. It is after all the white who must come to accept the black if the white is the racist. Second, in *The Cay*, the black hero Timothy is not at all concerned about being "accepted" by Philip, the white boy. Timothy makes no attempt to be other than he is and does not try to meet "white standards." The mistake seems to rest on confusing the fact that the story is told from the boy's *perspective* with the very different claim that the boy's *standards* constitute the approved norm. It is true that the boy comes to accept Timothy but this does not imply that the story contains the hidden message that whites are entitled to set the standards for Blacks. Third, and in support of this latter point, Philip is forced to admire, trust, and love Timothy because of the latter's ability and care. There is no suggestion that he has the right to bestow acceptance. Quite simply, the racist generalizations he has picked up are not borne out. Thus it is hard to see how the Council could arrive at the view that the book demeans the self-image of young black readers. Timothy does not need favors from anyone. He is the very model of independence and self-sufficiency.

The Cay makes no explicit mention of the fact that Philip comes to abandon his prejudice against blacks but a good writer has no need to spell matters out in this way. There are various indirect methods which can be used effectively, and here Theodore Taylor conveys this by the tone Philip adopts when thinking back to his experiences on the island with Timothy. An affectionate tone is not something which can be captured in a mechanical guideline. We can only recognize it by improving our reading skills and sensitivity. In the final line of the story, Philip imitates the accent and echoes the vocabulary of Timothy. If we ask how we are to know that this is not a patronizing white remark, the answer can only be that such a reading would be totally implausible in the context of the mood which the author has created. Even if the author had told us how the remark was to be taken, this would not be decisive. The interpretation would have to ring true in context.

Caricature and Stereotypes

Everyone will agree that the "happy-go-lucky, watermelon-eating Sambo" caricature, as the Guidelines put it, is offensive and racist, but in moving beyond this paradigm of stereotypes we must be cautious in following the recommendation that we look for generalizations "which in any way demean or ridicule characters because of their race . . ." Consider, first, an example from an adult book, Lawrence Durrell's portrait of Cyprus and Cypriots in *Bitter Lemons*. In the hilarious chapter entitled "How to buy a house," which puts one in mind of a knock-and-tumble, Keystone Cops sequence, we come across the following: "No Greek can sit still without fidgeting, tapping a foot or a pencil, jerking a knee, or making popping noises with his tongue. The Turk has a monolithic poise, an air of reptilian concentration and silence."[19]

It would be tempting here to fall into the intentional fallacy discussed earlier and make reference to Durrell's own attitudes to the country and its people to show that he is no racist. But no such move is necessary. It would simply be foolish to think that here we are encountering universal generalizations for all that the sentence begins "No Greek . . ." Durrell has noticed something, or thinks that he has, and exaggerates for effect. The effect is to set the stage for the antics which are to come when Sabri, the Turk, will have to work hard at maintaining his poise. Only the most naive reader could think that the book is trying to describe the buying and selling of houses, rather than giving the flavor of one particular transaction, liberally spiced for entertainment value.

Once again, it is important to have a feeling for the context as a whole in order to decide whether the remarks amount to subtle racism or good-natured fun. It is relevant here that nobody gets hurt, all enjoy themselves despite outward appearances, and the tone is light and cheerful. Durrell is as lost and bewildered as the other characters in the rapid turn of events. It is, in brief, a nonsense interlude in a book which has a serious and sombre undercurrent.

This is not to say, however, that nonsense can always be invoked to defeat the charge of bias. We may recall Austin's example of the person who pretends to behave vulgarly and thereby succeeds in behaving vulgarly.[20] By analogy, it seems to me that there is a problem with using examples such as "all women are feather-brained" in a logic text and claiming that such examples are merely silly. We cannot overlook the fact that there is, unfortunately, a stereotypical belief to this effect which prevents it from being seen as just silly.[21] The context in which such an example would be nothing but good-natured fun has not yet arrived. Yet we must be careful not to allow such cases to cause us to react inappropriately elsewhere.

An example of this occurs when the guidelines discuss *Pippi in the South Seas* by Astrid Lindgren. The book is one in a series by the Swedish writer who has created a nonsense character. Pippi is a young girl, possessed of amazing strength, who delights in making fools of all who encounter her. This is the main source of humor in the book. Gentlemen who think themselves distinguished, ladies who consider themselves very important, bungling crooks, and tiresome relatives, they are all cut down to size by Pippi's bizarre arguments and behavior. Everyone is fair game, except her two friends, and Pippi is invincible. We lose perspective if we pronounce, in the manner of the guidelines, that *Pippi in the South Seas* is anti-sexist but racist.[22] This rests apparently on the claim that a white girl guides foolish grownup Blacks. But this is a world in which everyone looks foolish. Certainly, Pippi's father is the great white chief of the south seas' island, but his name *is* King Efraim 1 Longstocking and the inscription commemorating his arrival on the island reads: "Over the great wide sea came our fat white chief. . . . May he remain just as fat and magnificent as when he came." This hardly suggests a relationship of white superiority. There is an equality of foolishness, and there is nothing more sinister to be read between the lines about blacks. It may be said, of course, that the situation lends itself to misrepresentation by racists even if it is not racist itself. This point certainly needs to be taken into account in making a decision about the book in a teaching context, and should be weighed against the point that children need to develop their own sense of judgment with respect to the distinction between what is, and what can be misrepresented as, racist.[23]

Education

The authors assert that "the guidelines are not meant to be prescriptive."[24] It is not clear, however, what this reassuring comment amounts to. If it means that the guidelines carry no implications for action, as a literal reading would suggest, then they have been misdescribed as guidelines and one wonders why the points have been called to the reader's attention at all. On the other hand, if it means that the rules are not fool-proof but must be applied with caution, several comments are called for. First, while it is true that every complexity cannot be built into a guideline without it becoming too intricate and cumbersome for practical use, nevertheless the present guidelines are overly simple and neglect certain elementary qualifications. Second, moreover, the cautionary advice notwithstanding, the guidelines are in fact applied in a simplistic and mechanical way to stories which are quite sophisticated. These two points together seem likely to foster the mistaken view that literature can be assessed by appeal to simple rules applied mechanically. This is surely miseducative. Third, and to make matters worse, the present guidelines do accurately identify *some* stories as racist, for example, *Bright April* and *The Matchlock Gun*,[25] thus creating the false view that the guidelines are adequate and reliable. It is vital, therefore, that students recognize the limitations of the guidelines with respect to other cases.

While the guidelines call attention to the importance of reading between the lines and appreciating what is conveyed without actually being said, they fail to do equal justice to the accompanying danger of reading in too much. If our students are to become critical readers, the point cannot be over-emphasized that interpretations must be supported. When we read between the lines, it remains true that our view needs to be defended in terms of what is and is not said. There is a very real danger of veering away from this fundamental aspect of criticism if students are encouraged to check out the author's background or to check the copyright date. At the very least, it needs to be pointed out that these suggestions may well lead us to "find" racism where none exists.[26] Again, students may be encouraged to watch for certain "loaded" words as long as it is clear that there is no *simple* move from the appearance of certain words to the charge of racism. A host of factors, including context, mood, character, humor, satire, and ambivalence, may enter in to complicate the judgment and the student must develop a sensitivity to the complexities of language use. Finally, certain words which are mistakenly thought to have a racist connotation are in fact normally quite innocent, though in particular contexts they might carry a racist meaning.

The two paragraphs immediately preceding discuss certain implications for literary education. It is equally important to see that certain issues in moral education are raised. We are, after all, dealing with the charge of racism, a very serious moral accusation. Morality requires that we treat others with respect, a requirement which the racist violates. Respect does not, of course, mean that we must refrain from criticism but it does mean that a full and fair consideration must be given before serious accusations are levelled. It is ironic, therefore, that the charge of racism is based on flimsy and superficial grounds in the guidelines. It is tragic that these grounds include some which seem likely to encourage racist attitudes. Children are urged to be suspicious of authors who are white and middle class, but this is the classic error of judging an individual by generalizations made about the group to which he or she belongs. The effect of the charge being bandied about may well be to rob the term of the seriousness which properly belongs to the concept.

The Council quite properly condemns the foisting of ideas onto children,[27] but their concern over indoctrination seems to be limited to opposing views which they find objectionable. They are less concerned about encouraging a critical examination of ideas which they subscribe to such as the belief that competition is bad.[28] It is not their admission that they are frankly advocating a particular kind of society which raises the spectre of indoctrination, for advocacy can take very different forms. What is vital, however, is that children have an opportunity to make up their own minds about controversial questions such as the merits of competition. If literature is to be employed to teach moral values, we will require teachers who have a more sophisticated grasp of moral issues than that displayed in the guidelines where, for example, competitiveness is portrayed as wholly evil.

The assumption here, however, that literature is to be a vehicle for moral education is one which calls for careful consideration.[29] If we seek the justification of literature solely in the moral lessons which it teaches, then we at once eliminate all that literature which does not raise or treat moral issues at all. The authors of the guidelines maintain that they are seeking "good values and good writing,"[30] and at first glance this seems unexceptionable. When, however, it is coupled with the independently false view that "a failure to work for change actually supports the status quo,"[31] then the way is open to ignore and even condemn a work whose primary merit is literary or aesthetic. If "good values" are identified with moral values, literary criticism will collapse into moral didacticism.

None of this is to endorse aestheticism, at least in its extreme form where aesthetic values are held to be supreme. Rather, it is to recognize what the guidelines tend to overlook, that aesthetic and moral values are different and this difference is not undermined, nor its importance diminished, by allowing that literature is capable of being the most powerful, morally educative force.[32] Certainly, too, there may be good moral reasons, especially perhaps in a multicultural society, for trying to ensure that children read books which portray characters from different racial groups. It is important, however, to recognize that when, in this way, a particular story is omitted, it is not because it is racist. It may be necessary to pass over a fine story in the interests of other criteria such as curricular balance and student self-image. Of course, the latter objective will not be met if what is substituted is not also fine from a literary point of view. Anything short of this will rapidly imply tokenism. Again, this shows the importance of a distinctive aesthetic standard.

Since aesthetic and moral values are different, however, it is clear that they may, on occasion, come into conflict. We may find, for example, that a story which has strong literary merit is marred by racist overtones or aspects which were not perhaps recognized by the author, or generally apparent, when the story first appeared. Blacks may be referred to in what are now, unmistakably, patronizing and demeaning ways. In deciding on the suitability of such a book, there is surely nothing for it but to exercise our judgment. Important factors here, further guidelines if you will, are the context in which our teaching occurs and the critical and emotional maturity of our students.

Concluding Comment

Guidelines can be useful when they are perceived as a checklist, designed to ensure that we will not neglect important factors when we are conducting a review. They cannot ensure that our judgments will be perfect, but they can increase the probability that vital considerations will be taken into account.[33]

There is always a danger, however, that guidelines will be viewed as a code which is taken as necessary and sufficient in formulating judgments.[34] Something like this has happened in the case of the guidelines under review, and this is particularly disturbing when the content of the guidelines is in any case seriously inadequate.

Postscript: 1993

In the years since this discussion was first published, the attack on excellent literature has continued unabated and is well documented. The ongoing problem can be illustrated with reference to a recent Canadian case. District 20 School Board in New Brunswick came under criticism in September 1991 from a community group in St. John for including in the high school curriculum Harper Lee's *To Kill A Mockingbird*. The group, known as PRUDE (Pride of Race, Unity, and Dignity through Education) took the view that the novel is offensive and racist. The issue was referred to the Minister of Education for resolution, and it is reassuring to be able to report now that "neither the Department of Education nor the District 20 School Board banned the novel; it continues to be included as an option on a list of approved resources for Senior High English Language Arts in the province of New Brunswick."[35]

Reassuring because, far from being racist, this wonderful story succeeds in showing what it is like to live in a community infected with racist attitudes, how innocent lives can be tragically destroyed by this virus. No fair-minded reader could fail to detect the high moral tone and sensitivity of the novel. If this book is judged to be racist, we have lost all contact with the real meaning of that concept and our words are idling. For thousands of young readers, I would say, this book has played a significant role in consciousness-raising at its best, by heightening the awareness of students to a serious and pervasive societal problem. In the hands of a sensitive teacher, it can be the vehicle for an educational experience with moral, social, aesthetic, and philosophical dimensions. If we cannot bring our students to appreciate such a novel by the end of their school experience, when they are already young adults, we should frankly confess that our efforts at education have failed.

Notes

1. *Guidelines for Selecting Bias-free Textbooks and Storybooks*, New York: Council on Interracial Books for Children, 1980. These guidelines are not now as frequently cited as they were in the mid-1980s, but the attitudes which they represent are still very common. When the Guidelines were published, it was stated that this work constituted the Council's most important contribution to that date. I am not aware that the guidelines have been repudiated despite the fact that they are seriously flawed. In the Acknowledgements to the Guidelines, it is stated that insights and perspectives have been drawn from various reviewers described as "members of oppressed groups." Perhaps this is an appropriate place to point out that membership in a particular group does not thereby confer the judgment necessary to assess literature. More sophisticated guidelines, such as the California State Department of Education Standards for Evaluation of Instructional Materials 1986, which have

appeared subsequently are also problematic, though they avoid the cruder mistakes of the *Guidelines* (For criticism of the California Standards, see my discussion in *What Makes A Good Teacher*, Althouse Press, 1993).

2. op. cit.: 2.

3. It is sometimes alleged that the distinction between the doctrine and the practice is artificial, but this objection really rests on the different grounds that the distinction sometimes has no practical value or that it may be dangerous to admit the distinction. See Sandra Bruneau, "Racism and teaching practices," in D. Cochrane and M. Schiralli (eds.), *Philosophy of Education: Canadian Perspectives,* Don Mills: Collier-Macmillan, 1982: 182-95.

4. Irving Thalberg, "Visceral racism," in R. Wasserstrom (ed.), *Today's Moral Problems,* New York: Macmillan, 1975: 187-204.

5. *Guidelines*, op. cit.: 6.

6. op. cit.: 26.

7. op. cit.: 12.

8. Paula Fox, *The Slave Dancer,* New York: Bradbury Press, 1973: 72.

9. Incidentally, it is not true that the horrors of the slave trade are shown in such a way that "no young reader was left with respect for black people." One of the few, genuinely kind actions in the book occurs when the boy is searching for his fife in the hold where it had been deliberately dropped by one of the hands. A young black boy returns it to Jessie. When the two boys are later hiding in the dark hold, it is the same black boy who shows Jessie how to obtain moisture from the damp surface of the casks, clearly an intelligent solution to a problem.

10. *Guidelines*, op. cit.: 7-8.

11. Shakespeare, Sonnet 147.

12. *Guidelines*, op. cit.: 10.

13. Aristotle, *Poetics*, Section 24.

14. *Guidelines*, op. cit.: 13.

15. op. cit.: 18.

16. op. cit.: 12.

17. op. cit.: 19-20. Sharon Bell Mathis is quoted in the *Guidelines* as having asked the question: "If your children were Black, would you give them *The Slave Dancer* to read?" Surely, the obvious answer here is an emphatic "Yes!"

18. op. cit.: 11.

19. Lawrence Durrell, *Bitter Lemons,* London: Faber and Faber, 1957: 48.

20. J. L. Austin, "Pretending," in Donald F. Gustafson (ed.), *Essays in Philosophical Psychology*, London: Macmillan, 1967: 105.

21. See Maryann Ayim and Barbara Houston, "A conceptual analysis of sexism and sexist education," in Cochrane and Schiralli (eds.), *Philosophy of Education: Canadian Perspectives,* op. cit.: 145-70.

22. *Guidelines*, op. cit.: 16.

23. There is some serious doubt as to whether or not the authors of the *Guidelines* actually read *Pippi in the South Seas*. First, there is no incident in the text, as far as I can see, where Pippi "guides foolish grown-up Blacks." Second, the illustration

from the story reproduced in the *Guidelines*, which I assume is taken to represent racism, actually shows King Efraim 1 Longstocking (a white man) looking extremely foolish as he sits on his throne (The author of the novel makes quite a good conceptual joke to show that we are not to take his authority too seriously: "King Efraim had been away from his ruling duties for quite a while, and now he started to rule with all his might." Shades of Lewis Carroll!

24. *Guidelines,* op. cit.: 2.

25. Walter D. Edmonds, *The Matchlock Gun,* New York: Dodd, Mead and Company, 1941. Even here, however, the short account given in the guidelines is misleading. The mother does "lure" certain Indians to their deaths, but the context is one of self-defense. The fault is that of omission.

26. See Antony Flew, *Thinking About Thinking,* Glasgow: Fontana/Collins, 1975: 58-63. Flew labels the fallacy in question *The Subject/Motive Shift.* It is a form of ad hominem.

27. *Guidelines,* op. cit.: 11.

28. op. cit.: 19.

29. Others have expressed the need for caution in this context. R. S. Peters has pointed out the risk of distortion if literature is just used for other purposes, such as promoting sensitivity. See his "'Mental health' as an educational aim," in T. H. B. Hollins (ed.), *Aims in Education,* Manchester: Manchester University Press, 1964: 88. And R. M. Hare has shown that literature can easily, yet misleadingly, suggest that a generally accepted moral principle ought to be abandoned. See his *Moral Thinking,* Oxford: Clarendon Press, 1981: 48.

30. *Guidelines,* op. cit.: 21.

31. op. cit., p. 13.

32. See, for example, Iris Murdoch, *The Sovereignty of Good Over Other Concepts,* London: Cambridge University Press, 1967: 15.

33. See Donna Kerr, *Educational Policy: Analysis, Structure and Justification,* New York: David McKay, 1976: 180-1.

34. See Jack Clarke, "Reference ethics - Do we need them?" in *The Reference Librarian 4,* 1982: 25-30. Clarke switches from talk of guidelines to talk of codes without noticing that a significant change has occurred.

35. Personal communication from the Minister of Education in New Brunswick, September 15, 1992.

8
Reflections on Teaching

The concept of teaching is a central notion in philosophy of education and it is important for teachers to have a full and adequate conception of teaching at their disposal. This chapter offers an analysis of teaching, a normative account of teaching, and considers some empirical claims which have been made about teaching.

The Need for Reflection

Faced with the imminent prospect of having to teach a class for the first time, it is no surprise when student teachers favor the acquisition of basic survival skills over the exploration of philosophical questions, even when these are related to the teaching context. Nevertheless, there are reasons why student teachers need to reflect philosophically on the enterprise of teaching, on what teaching is and ought to be and on what research on teaching has to offer, and these reasons can have a bearing on one's ultimate survival as a teacher. Chief among these is simply the fact that the way in which we think of teaching has an influence on the way in which we teach. Constraints and opportunities emerge from our theoretical framework. To remove the constraint is at once to create an opportunity. Philosophy has an important role to play in permitting such opportunities to present themselves.

Obviously enough, teaching will suffer if teachers lack certain practical skills. The relevance of methods classes is widely acknowledged. It is not so readily appreciated that teaching can be adversely affected in other ways also. We can, for example, slip into a rather narrow view of teaching and arbitrarily limit what we see as possible, with the result that certain methods or objectives do not arise for us as live options. Another pitfall is to accept uncritically what passes for good teaching without asking what teaching, at its finest, might be like and whether there are certain ideals which should guide teaching. Finally, we can allow ourselves to be influenced by research findings without pausing to ask searching questions about the interpretation and application of these findings.

Philosophy has a contribution to make in each of these areas. There is such an enormous literature, however, that there can be no attempt here to summarize the field, nor to explore the complexities which have arisen in any detail. Our task must be more illustrative, inspired by important suggestions in the literature, as we try to substantiate the claims made on behalf of philosophy. Any attempt to do this, however, is likely to encounter a certain initial scepticism based on general considerations which need to be addressed directly.

The first kind of doubt is raised by Robin Barrow who suggests that certain concepts, including teaching, are relatively unproblematic.[1] We know well enough what teaching is, and we do not need the kind of sustained, conceptual inquiry into teaching which might be needed with other concepts. Barrow is not dogmatic about this and concedes that there will be room for disagreement about which concepts are unproblematic. Others have certainly agreed with him in this connection, notably Jacques Barzun who turned with great dispatch from the endless controversy about education to what he saw as the more manageable topic of teaching.[2] It is not easy, however, to declare that a concept just is inherently unproblematic. Those which, we may think, *ought* to be can be made problematic as they become enmeshed in theories and slogans. When, elsewhere, Barrow sees the need to argue that teachers cannot be both non-directive and teaching,[3] this is because he believes that others have become confused about the nature of teaching. Perhaps we have only raised a dust where otherwise we might see clearly, but now conceptual clarification is needed if only to recall us to common sense.

A very different objection arises from those who believe that conceptual inquiry is ultimately futile. Far from being unproblematic, the concepts prove unamenable to analysis. In the words of a recent and fair-minded critic, counter-examples arise to defeat any analysis.[4] Here the objection is not that the approach taken by philosophers of education in the recent past was too linguistic or too arbitrary. These are faults of conceptual inquiry as practised, not as such. Talk of stagnation and futility, however, suggests that the whole enterprise is in vain. On this point, however, it is worth recalling the remark of Etienne Gilson that even where definitions are not possible, it can be profitable to attempt them.[5] Perhaps more was promised in the heyday of analytical philosophy of education than was, or could have been, delivered. But now we need to ask what was learned along the way.

Although there was a tremendous burst of conceptual inquiry concerning teaching in the twenty year period from 1955 to 1975, it would be a mistake to think that earlier philosophers of education had not addressed these issues. Certainly, some analytical philosophers of education managed to give the impression that earlier contributions had been almost entirely wrongheaded. The proper task of philosophy, the careful demarcation of concepts, had degenerated, we were told, into the formulation of high-level directives,[6] presumably more airy than lofty. This was a hopeless caricature, of course, but Dewey, Russell, and others were effectively written off. Enthusiasm for conceptual analysis has now waned considerably, and former devotees are anxious to dissociate themselves from the errors of misguided youth.[7] Conceptual clarification is dismissed as so much idle chatter. It is a kind of sport, diverting at times, but pointless and often boring. No doubt there is an element of poetic justice in this sudden reversal of fortune, but we are perilously close to concluding that if conceptual inquiry is not all important, it is not important at all. Such an about-face will not serve to recover the tradition of philosophy of education, and might lead us to throw out the achievements of the analytic period along with the dregs.

The Polymorphous Nature of Teaching

Even if we are inclined to think that the notion of teaching is straightforward, we soon encounter comments and questions about teaching which force us to reflect on our everyday assumptions. In particular, we encounter the suggestion that something or other cannot be taught, and it is clear that the claim is not based on experience, nor is it one which is to be tested in an experimental way. An answer can only be found, if at all, by thinking about the idea of teaching and about whatever is said to be unteachable. Socrates at times took the view that virtue could not be taught, partly because it was not knowledge and partly because those who professed to be teachers of virtue were themselves confused about the matter.[8] Kant held that while rules could be taught, judgment could not. Judgment is something which comes with practice but no one can teach another person a sense of judgment.[9] Jacques Barzun cited tolerance, democracy, and citizenship as improper objects of teaching. These cannot be taught, Barzun held, because they are attitudes not subject matter.[10] And a recent textbook for High School politics courses asserts that no one can be taught to think. At best, a few suggestions can be offered to the learner.[11]

These claims run counter to widely held views. If we judge by the enormous efforts which have been made in recent years to develop educational programs in moral education and critical thinking, one would have to conclude that there is a strong belief that such matters can be taught and are among the most important items in any list of educational aims. Of course, those who deny that teaching is possible with respect to these objectives, do not mean to suggest that virtue, judgment, and the ability to think are not worthwhile, only that they must be acquired in some other way. Favorite answers would include practice, experience, personal discovery, and example.

Before exploring this issue and the questions it raises about teaching, we need to ask if anything really hinges on this disagreement. After all, everyone agrees that the achievements in question are desirable, and even those who exclude the possibility of teaching are often prepared to say that the teacher *as a person* is instrumental in their emergence. Barzun, for example, concedes that such achievements occur as by-products of good teaching. They come from a teacher, not from a course.[12] It begins to sound suspiciously like a verbal dispute, and a trivial issue. It may be, however, that matters of consequence lurk behind such a seemingly superficial dispute. If teachers define their work primarily as teaching, then what they attempt will be related to what they view as possible and relevant given their understanding of this concept.

If we ask what is basic to our idea of teaching, it seems clear that we cannot begin to explain it without introducing the idea of learning. We know that people can learn things without the benefit of teaching, and so there is a clear sense in which learning does not require teaching. This is not always clear in practice, however, where we can slip into the view that learning only goes on in the context of teaching and this risk is increased if we define the learners as pupils. If this mistake is avoided, there remains the related one of thinking that the only *worthwhile* learning is that which results from teaching. One serious practical consequence of this is a failure to utilize in our teaching what the student has learned independently.

Teaching, however, does require learning in the sense that learning of some sort is the objective at which teaching aims. Certainly, the central case for teachers, leaving aside team teaching, is that in which **one person sets out to act in such a way that what is to be learned can be learned by others from what he or she does.** Many different kinds of learning may be intended, from carpentry to calculus, but that some intended learning outcome is necessary can be seen from the nonsense which results otherwise. Think, for example, of teaching in an otherwise empty classroom, or in a language foreign to, and beyond the comprehension of, the students. In a different case, what sense could we make of setting out to teach someone what that person already understands and, therefore, cannot learn?

Of course, all of these examples can be *made* intelligible, but in each case this is done by smuggling in the objective of learning.[13] For example, the room might be empty because the teacher is recording a lesson for educational television. The use of a foreign language might be designed to foster appreciation of the situation of a newly arrived immigrant who must grapple with a new language. Again, we may aim at a deeper understanding of what a student in some way already grasps, at pursuing further implications of ideas already covered. (The conceptual point is not a reason to exclude review periods from the business of teaching.) These cases, however, can now be understood as teaching precisely because we have found a way to reintroduce learning as an objective.

Our central case involves teaching others, so the notion of teaching oneself falls outside it and should, I suggest, be considered a derivative form of teaching though one which is important in its own way. It is not our primary example of teaching because it derives its status as a kind of teaching by analogy with the case where one person teaches someone else. When we teach ourselves, we are in effect learning on our own without the benefit of teaching. But we set about the task in ways which resemble to some extent the situation in which we have someone else as a teacher. Perhaps we have a teach-yourself book, where another person is in the background as teacher. Or we set ourselves drills and tasks as a teacher might. Our learning does not just happen, as it often does when we learn on our own, so there is some further resemblance to the standard case. But there are important differences too. We cannot very well explain something to ourselves, yet explanation is a common form that teaching takes. So teaching oneself is a kind of half-way house, but an important notion if it serves to remind us of the need for learners to start to assume greater responsibility for their own learning, and to leave their teachers behind.[14]

Analogies are also at work in many of the cases which suggest that teaching can be unintentional. There is, for example, a view, found in Wordsworth and others, that portrays nature as teaching moral virtue more effectively than the philosophers. This is a dramatic way of marking the occasion of one's learning and of identifying the experiences which elicited it. It is *as if* we had learned from a teacher, but this is a metaphorical extension of literal meaning. We understand the point, and it is effective, because we draw on the case of one person teaching another. In other cases, however, we are, at most, just a step away from our central case of teaching. We sometimes hold that some persons are teaching others, perhaps their children, just by the way in which they behave, with no reference to any intentions.[15] In such a case, we find example, repetition, authority, and other common features of teaching situations which make a sharp division or boundary seem somewhat arbitrary here. Teaching is, to some extent, a vague notion, and one can only make it more precise than it really is through stipulation.

What is more important than deciding exactly where to draw the line, however, is recognizing that in teaching one thing many other kinds of learning may be going on. John Dewey made the point very effectively when he exposed what he called the greatest of all pedagogical fallacies, namely the belief that the person is only learning the particular thing being studied at the time.[16] We set out, let us say, to teach history or physics and we may or may not have much success. But perhaps students are learning that these subjects are boring, or that we ourselves are unenthusiastic because we are out of our depth. There are many possible results in the form of attitudes, interests, traits, and inferences which may not have been intended, but which can be attributed in some way to our work as teachers. The hidden curriculum is often concealed from teachers also, and Dewey's warning may serve to prompt us to examine our teaching more critically. The concept of unintentional teaching may prepare us to find in the results of our efforts more than we had bargained for.[17]

These possible results also serve to remind us how *extensive* the notion of learning is. We may think immediately of knowledge, as it seems Socrates did at times, when we ask what can be learned, but clearly learning can go beyond knowledge even if this is understood to include both skills and information. Students can learn to appreciate something, to take an interest, to become more open-minded or critical, to look for problems, to tolerate criticism, and so on; but none of these is the same as acquiring knowledge. To be open-minded, for example, is not to possess a certain type of knowledge, but to acquire an attitude with respect to knowledge. To have learned to look for problems is to have developed a certain habit and also perhaps to have realized that something is worth doing. A limited notion of what can be learned breeds a limited notion of teaching, one which helps to explain Passmore's law that all subjects tend towards an instructional state.[18] We forget what can be learned from them, and thereby undermine our own efforts to teach them well.

There is a tendency, however, to insist that such things as attitudes can only be caught or picked up. They cannot be taught.[19] What lies behind this idea, I believe, is an unreasonably narrow view of the forms which teaching can take. The objection fails to recognize that teaching activities are polymorphous. When it is said that only suggestions can be offered, it is clear that the contrast is with a rule, formula, or theory which can be given in instruction so that what is to be learned is explicit and complete. Surely, however a good suggestion, at the right time, may be the very thing which will help us to learn. The teacher will need judgment to know when the time is right, and judgment may well grow out of practice. But we can be set to practise in relevant ways by others with experience who know how and when to offer useful comments. If successful learning here is less predictable than in direct instruction, this only confirms Spinoza's view that all excellent things are as difficult as they are rare.[20]

Sometimes it is objected that we cannot properly speak of learning or teaching in these cases because the outcomes basically *happen* to people. They are not *achievements* on the part of the learner.[21] Of course, it is admitted that they do not *just* happen, at least normally; they are only likely to occur in certain circumstances. Nevertheless, they are a kind of contagion. Against this view, we need to remember that we cannot sensibly deny that a person has learned something even though he or she was not trying to learn that thing, and perhaps *could not* have tried to learn it. When we notice or realize something, a mistake perhaps, or an implication, there is no doubt that we have learned something although we did not set out to learn it. We can be struck by an idea, but it would be very odd to claim that we were trying to be struck by it.[22] When we learn a lesson the hard way, perhaps by having our unlocked car stolen, we could hardly set out to learn this without somehow having learned the lesson already. So learning can happen, but it is learning nonetheless and may be immensely important.

If the learner cannot claim an *achievement* because he or she is overtaken in this way, perhaps some other person can! What was to be learned, the attitude, interest, habit, or ability, was learned *because* someone else behaved in a certain way. An example was set, an attitude displayed, an enthusiasm was evident, with the result that learning was fostered. These cases are not open to the sort of objection brought against B. O. Smith's analysis of teaching as a system of actions intended to induce learning.[23] Philip Jackson points out that this account is broad enough to cover giving medicine to a hyperactive child so that he or she might benefit from instruction.[24] But here, of course, the learning which follows is only made possible *by* what is done. The child does not learn *from* what is done. We can look further than Jackson does for a generic account of teaching, as I have indicated. Jackson wonders why we should bother. The answer is simply that such an account can serve to undermine a restricted view of teaching.

Teaching aims at learning but does not always succeed. The fact that it is not always causally efficacious, however, is not a reason to conclude that there is no causal relationship here. Gary Fenstermacher warns us against being easily lulled into thinking that one causes the other just because there is a conceptual relationship between teaching and learning. He concludes that learning is not an effect that follows from teaching as a cause.[25] Certainly we need to recognize that teaching can fail to produce the desired learning; but often it *is* successful, and the student's learning results because teaching was effective. No doubt other factors were also necessary, but the teaching was a causal factor, either a further necessary condition or a sufficient condition given the other factors present.

Fenstermacher is anxious to revise our general account of teaching from one which assumes a causal connection between teaching and learning to one which views teaching as that which *enables* others to study successfully. One central task of teaching, he insists, is to enable the student to perform the tasks of learning. He links this with teaching the student to learn how to learn. Now, this suggestion fits in well with the view that learning is a more extensive notion than we sometimes think. We sometimes overlook the possibility of learning that which will enable one to go on learning on one's own. Learning is a task as well as an achievement, and teaching can enable us to pursue the task. This is conceptually accurate, and worth pointing out.

It does not follow from this, however, that the causal view is mistaken or that the generic account needs to be revised. We might believe that the most important kind of teaching is that which leads to learning how to learn, but that would take us out of the conceptual into the normative realm, and Fenstermacher makes it clear that his claim is conceptual. The problem is that he does not restrict himself to the claim that *one* central task of teaching is to enable what he terms "studenting" to occur.[26] He also claims that this is *the* task of teaching. As we have seen, however, teaching can also aim at producing the sort of learning which happens when a student is struck by an idea. Here the notion of a prior task eventuating in an achievement for *the student* does not properly apply. In this case, learning happens and it is properly attributed to teaching.

Even in those cases where learning results as a genuine *achievement*, it may be proper to speak of learning being *imparted*. When an explanation is offered by a teacher, the student may be willing to pay attention and to follow the account. The teaching, however, need not set out to *enable* these tasks to occur, it may happily *presuppose* them in certain cases. An explanation is given, but it is not implied that the learner does *nothing*. When a student understands an explanation, learning as an achievement results and it is produced by teaching. Explaining after all is one of the forms which teaching takes.

Furthermore, in those cases where the aim of teaching *is* to enable the student to pursue certain tasks, becoming able to pursue them is also something which has to be learned. We are able to undertake certain tasks when we have *learned* to do so. The achievement is to be in a position, and perhaps willing, to undertake the task. Learning as an achievement has not been eliminated, but is to be seen at the same time as a step towards *further* achievements rather than a final end. So even with a recognition of studenting, as Fenstermacher puts it, as a central aim of teaching, we still retain that generic sense of teaching as acting in such a way that what is to be learned can be learned from what is done. The only difference concerns *what* is to be learned. If these results can be attributed to teaching, then a causal account still applies.[27]

A Normative Perspective on Teaching

The intense preoccupation with conceptual analysis which characterized philosophy of education in the recent past meant that attempts to set out, in normative terms, ideals which teaching ought to satisfy were dismissed as "high-level directives." Traditional "philosophical" reflection on teaching was thought to have missed the mark. Instead of inquiring into the meaning of teaching, where argument could be brought to bear, it became embroiled in endless and unprofitable controversy about values on which philosophers had no special competence to pronounce.[28] This extreme view is now in retreat, and perhaps even old-fashioned. But it remains important to see *how* philosophy is relevant to the normative debate.

The first contribution arises in response to the fashionable view that idealized conceptions of teaching, while splendid no doubt, are mythical. The concept of the hidden curriculum reaches beyond the claim that in teaching one lesson you may also be teaching another, to the claim that the very activity of teaching itself inescapably contains certain lessons *whatever* is being taught. Sometimes this appears as the claim that the pupil learns that only what is taught is valuable;[29] elsewhere as the claim, a paradox of sorts, that before teaching takes place at all, we are taught what teaching means.[30] The inevitable lesson is that some are authorized to speak and others forced to listen. If these claims were true, ideals such as freedom, open-mindedness, and independence would be spurious, and any normative recommendation would founder. Ought, after all, implies can.

The initial role of philosophy here is to show that the alleged inevitability is itself spurious. It is one thing to claim that it is always *possible* that a student will learn that the only worthwhile learning is that which one's teachers provide, and quite another to assert that this outcome is *inevitable*. First, it is not the only conceivable inference, hence it is not logically inevitable. Second, taken as a causal claim it is open to challenge on empirical grounds and capable of being offset by other factors. For example, the danger can be openly discussed to ensure that it does not occur by default. As teachers, we can actually employ the hidden curriculum to advantage by showing, in our behavior, that we *do* value the knowledge the student has which we have *not* taught.

The inequality involved in the teacher/student relationship, which the earlier discussion of self-teaching and its limits shows to be necessary, is supposed to generate the paradoxical conclusion that, before we can begin to promote open-mindedness and critical thinking in our teaching, our normative aspirations are scuttled at the outset by the authoritarian relationship implicit in *any* teaching. If this were only intended to promote consciousness-raising by alerting us to the possibility of our best efforts being undermined, it would be unexceptionable. As a would-be logical barrier, however, it crumbles on critical examination. First, even if it were true that teaching presupposed an authoritarian framework, there is no reason in principle why teaching could not prepare the ground for an assault on that very framework. Experience might, and in fact does, I believe, show that certain approaches to teaching are more conducive than others to the emergence of autonomous thought. Second, moreover, while the teaching relationship does imply that the teacher is in some sense an authority with respect to the relevant subject matter, this is not at all the same as reading authoritarianism and deference into every situation. This is conceptual sleight of hand. Of course, if the student is studying at all with a teacher, he or she is necessarily attending in some way to what the teacher says or does. This need not, however, be slavish and uncritical, and if it were the teacher could discourage it.

Teaching does attempt to construct a certain framework of beliefs, assumptions, attitudes, and expectations, but it is not the existence of a framework *per se* which threatens normative ideals such as creativity, autonomy, or critical reflection. A framework-free education, in any case, makes no sense. The crucial question, however, is whether or not teaching sets out to encourage students to demand evidence for claims and to accept the possibility that longstanding beliefs may have to be abandoned. In this way, long-term objectives need to be taken into account in the assessment of teaching before the charge of indoctrination can be levelled.[31]

If a non-authoritarian conception of teaching makes sense, as it surely does, what is to be said in favor of such a view? Here we come to the second task of philosophy in the normative area, that of setting out and defending certain ideals which teaching must pursue. The fact that these are ideals is no reason to conclude that they have no bearing on the practical business of teaching. If they cannot be completely realized, teachers can look for ways in which they are more closely approximated.

When Bertrand Russell, for example, suggested that teaching requires humility, he was attempting to characterize an attitude which philosophers of education since Socrates have judged to be central. Russell recognized the need for philosophical comment here because the suggestion is somewhat paradoxical, as the preceding discussion of authoritarianism suggests. He captured the puzzle by speaking of "an unaccountable humility – a humility not easily defensible on any rational ground, and yet somehow nearer to wisdom than the easy self-confidence of many parents and teachers."[32] The teacher knows so much more than the child. Why then the need for humility? Part of the answer, as Russell saw, lies in the Socratic reminder that the teacher is capable of inflicting great damage on his or her students. Socrates pointed out that knowledge cannot be carried away in a parcel: "When you have paid for it you must receive it into the soul: you go away having learned it and are benefited or harmed accordingly."[33] The skills of the teacher, like other skills, can be put to good or bad use. Moreover, as we have seen, the actions of any teacher can have unintended consequences. The teacher needs to be conscious of the position of trust he or she occupies, and seek to teach in such a way that students become able to make their own informed and impartial choices.

The concept of trust brings to mind the sorry Keegstra episode,[34] where humility was noticeably absent and swaggering self-confidence the defiant note. This fatal sense of one's own infallible judgment underscores the importance of humility. Socrates was the first to challenge the smugness of teachers concerning their own mastery of the subject they professed to teach. His target, of course, was the Sophists who needed to take the first step in the direction of wisdom by recognizing their own limited knowledge. It is the conceit of wisdom which leads Protagoras, for example, to believe that he is better than anyone else at helping others to acquire a good and noble character.[35] The fundamental problem with this attitude, as Socrates makes clear elsewhere,[36] is that we cannot advise someone how to attain virtue if we ourselves do not understand what it is.

The general point being made here applies in any subject area. All views are capable of being revised, and even if our teachers have a sound academic preparation (as Keegstra did not), there would still be a need to recognize that one's beliefs are vulnerable. In this way, humility is part of the attitude of open-mindedness.[37] Certainly, as Dewey was quick to point out, the teacher is the member of the group with "larger experience and riper wisdom;"[38] but the "learned man should also still be a learner."[39] This will involve not only adding to one's store of knowledge, but also coming to realize that certain of one's beliefs have to be abandoned. The kind of humility which amounts to open-mindedness involves healthy self-criticism and is not at all the same as neurotic doubt.

The teacher who recognizes the rights of the student and the fallibility of claims to knowledge is presumably someone prepared to teach in a *critical manner*.[40] The student is encouraged to ask for reasons and the teacher is prepared to respond to them. All this implies that the teacher's ideas are not beyond criticism. Dewey deplored the situation in which "children are hushed up when they ask questions; their exploring and investigating activities are inconvenient and hence they are treated like nuisances."[41] It *is* a nuisance if we adopt the view that teaching is nothing more than the efficient transmission of information from teacher to student. A critical approach, however, demands that we "respect the student's intellectual integrity and capacity for independent judgment."[42]

The character of this attitude can be illustrated if we take note of the ambiguity in Quintilian's remark in the *Institutio Oratoria* (Book 2), that the teacher must be ready to answer questions. A teacher might be prepared to answer questions seeking information, but unwilling to entertain questions which raise objections with respect to the ideas being advanced in the lesson. The critical manner requires a willingness to accept the second kind of question also, and such an attitude amounts to respecting the student as an independent source of ideas. Russell spoke of *reverence* in this connection and viewed education as enabling students to choose intelligently. All too often, in practice, students are viewed as the potter views the clay, and their questions meet with dogma or stony silence.[43]

The concept of respect is completely misunderstood when it is thought to imply a teaching situation in which any and every student response calls for acceptance by the teacher.[44] There is some evidence apparently that this is the most frequent teacher response, one that implies that the student's comment is correct or appropriate, but which stops short of praise. Many teachers, it seems, *never* indicate that an answer is incorrect or inappropriate. Textbooks for teachers sometimes explicitly recommend the acceptance response, especially with respect to divergent questions.[45] In fact, in the literature on questioning as a teaching strategy, one of the most neglected areas is what we might call the *challenge* question where the student is required to support what he or she has just said.[46] The uncritical acceptance of student responses *fails* to show respect precisely because it does not take the responses seriously. If the responses are treated as equally useful and interesting, they are not being evaluated and considered. *Any* response will receive the same treatment.

This example actually illustrates a more general mistake which one encounters, namely that normative ideals are interpreted as directly implying procedural rules which can be read off in a straightforward way. When it is said, to take another example, that a classroom should manifest a spirit of discussion, this is to state a normative ideal about the importance of teachers and students being willing to listen seriously to the ideas of others and being prepared to reconsider their own views. We move too quickly, however, if this normative ideal is translated into a procedural recommendation in favor of discussion methods where the latter are interpreted as eschewing formal instruction. The fact is that a great many teaching strategies can display a spirit of discussion.

The result is that we fail to do justice to ideals in practice because we impose arbitrary constraints on their expression. We recognize, for example, the importance of teaching in an open-minded manner, but we make the mistake of concluding that certain actions necessarily violate this norm. It has been maintained recently, as we have seen earlier, that the use of the word *prove* in the science classroom demonstrates a lack of open-mindedness.[47] What has happened here is a failure to understand the nature of the normative ideal in question. Our ideals are bound to suffer if we do not pause to think critically about the concepts which give them expression. In this case, it is a failure to recognize that it is not the words we use but the way in which we use them which is decisive. It is the attitude which lies behind the word which determines whether or not this ideal is met.

The Numbers Game

To talk sense, said Whitehead, is to talk in quantities.[48] Generations of educational researchers have shown that they have taken this remark to heart. A massive amount of quantitative research has been undertaken in an attempt to determine what makes an effective teacher. Depressingly, however, many believe that we are no nearer to being able to offer firm evidence in support of preferred approaches.[49] Disenchantment has set in concerning quasi-experimental research modeled on the natural sciences, and interest has centred of late on qualitative research with its emphasis on description, interpretation, case studies, fieldwork, and particular circumstances. John Dewey, however, ought to have made all of us nervous about either/or choices. Quantitative research findings continue to appear and require an intelligent response from the teacher.

For example, it has been held since at least the time of Socrates that asking questions can be an effective teaching strategy. Yet it is also apparent to many teachers that their efforts in this direction are frustrated. Often few answers are forthcoming and the Socratic model degenerates into one in which the teacher answers his or her own questions. Some years ago, Mary Budd Rowe examined this problem and discovered that, after asking a question, the teacher would wait one second or less for a student to answer. Moreover, once the student had responded, the teacher would wait less than one second before commenting on the response. Rowe conducted an experiment to see what would happen if the teacher extended the wait time after asking a question and after the student had responded.[50]

The results were impressive. The length of student responses increased as did the number of unsolicited student responses. There was evidence of more speculative and confident responses, and slow learners made a greater contribution as teachers discovered that they had been giving these students *less* time to respond. All of this is carefully measured and dramatically represented in graphs showing the speech pattern in the classroom before and after wait time is extended. These results, however, do *not* translate into a rule-like formula which can be mechanically applied in the classroom. We can agree with Rowe that one second is hardly enough, but teachers will need to exercise their own judgment in deciding how long to wait. What the research does is create awareness of a phenomenon and demonstrate how it can be altered. It puts the teacher in a better position to make an intelligent judgment.

A philosophical perspective can complement the teacher's efforts in this regard. Increasing confidence on the part of the students was measured in Rowe's experiment by fewer voice inflections. But when does confidence shift into complacency, and speculation into idle digression? Here we need more than a simplistic behavioral criterion to guide us. An overall sense of one's educational objectives is necessary if good judgments are to be made. Rowe noticed that verbal rewards from the teacher tended to offset the benefits of wait time and promote the inflected voice response. She recommended "near neutral verbal rewards," whatever that may mean.[51] The problem here, of course is that we are not just teaching the subject matter involved in the question but also attitudes. There will surely be times when the teacher will want to burst in enthusiastically given a certain response without observing the requisite pause or the nearly neutral tone. The teacher needs to remember also that techniques can backfire if their use is all too obviously calculating, and can pall as they become commonplace. Dewey warned against the blind observance of rule and routine, and noted that "the machine teacher . . . makes his school a mere machine shop."[52]

Recent empirical research by J. T. Dillon has severely challenged the tradition we have inherited from Socrates with respect to questions as a teaching strategy, claiming that a question is more limiting than a statement.[53] This claim to some extent reflects an alleged *conceptual* difference between a question and a statement, but the main purpose is to make an empirical claim buttressed with solid evidence. Dillon has made a detailed study of classroom interaction comparing and contrasting the consequences of questions posed by the teacher with the use of alternative strategies such as declarative statements. With precise results set out in charts and tables, Dillon concludes that teacher questions *prevent* discussion. Students respond for twice as long to non-question alternatives, and in addition raise their own questions and offer speculations going beyond the reading.[54] Contrary to Rowe, he claims that the pace of the questions makes no difference.

Dillon suggests that further studies be conducted to see if his results can be falsified. The question, however, is whether or not *any* empirical research can show that questions are more effective than statements. Dillon's own conclusions have become more definite over the years: from his tentative view in 1979 that non-question alternatives might be useful now and then; to his 1985 view that questions simply foil discussion and non-question alternatives foster it. The former view presents the teacher with a suggestion, whereas the latter makes a law-like generalization. To make the comparison, however, one would have to *judge* that the tone of the questions and alternatives is similar, that the teachers are equally keen to make their strategies work, and are equally talented at posing *appropriate* questions or framing alternatives *at the right moment*. These factors cannot be read off from class transcripts in the same objective way as length of response. Moreover, if it is true that questions have been over-emphasized, then alternatives presently have the advantage of novelty.

We may be tempted to regard the results as decisive because simplistic, *conceptual* reasons suggest that we really should not be surprised. A question is thought to tell one what kind of answer to give, whereas a statement is supposed to leave the response open. But if questions can *limit*, statements can *lead*. Everything depends upon the *kind* of question or statement, the *context* in which it occurs, and the *way* in which it is put. Contrary to Dillon, statements are not *intrinsically* more surprising than questions. In the hands of a good teacher, a question need *not* say "Supply this bit of information and stop." It may be made clear that the presuppositions of a question are themselves open to challenge in just the same way as the positive assertions in a statement. We also need to resist the notion that attitudes can be determined in a purely formal way by identifying the kind of comment a teacher makes, for example an indirect question rather than a direct one. An indirect question such as "I'd like to hear more about that" *might* be encouraging and supportive (though it might *also* be threatening); but "I'd like to see you prove that," said in a certain tone, might convey a very different message.

Despite the reservations which empirical researchers themselves often express, the search continues for evidence that some particular strategy is more effective than others. In recent years, one approach to teaching which caught the imagination of teachers in Britain and North America arose in the context of dealing with controversial material. The Humanities Curriculum Project began in England in 1967 and adopted a teaching strategy designed to protect the student from the teacher's own biases. This strategy came to be known as procedural neutrality which meant essentially that the teacher was to be neutral in the classroom with respect to the substantive issue being discussed, but committed to standards of argumentation and respect for evidence. The teacher, in effect, was to serve as a neutral chairperson as the students discussed the controversial topic.[55]

It would be a great mistake to believe that the debate over the Humanities Curriculum Project was side-tracked by a verbal dispute. Lawrence Stenhouse suggested at one point that impartiality or objectivity would have been a better choice of word than neutrality. These other concepts, it must be noted, do not necessarily imply that the teacher is constrained from presenting to the class his or her own sincerely held point of view. This constraint, however, was built into the strategy adopted by the Project.[56] Indeed, it is by contrast with such a possibility that the distinctive strategy of the Project stands out. Those philosophers who defended the possibility of the teacher sharing his or her views with the students also accepted the values of impartiality and objectivity.

Philosphers who raised such points were strongly condemned for ignoring the "empirical reality in the classroom." They had, as one caustic comment put it, not allowed their minds to be clouded by looking at the available evidence.[57] It was allowed that, from a philosophical point of view, the idea of a teacher giving his or her view and being seen to remain open to criticism was impeccable. It was claimed, however, that observation shows that it does not seem to be possible to satisfy this in practice.[58] Experience shows, we were told, that it is "almost insuperably difficult."[59] But how could research show this in any generalizable way? The Humanities Curriculum Project conceded that situational verifiability is necessary. In other words, teachers need to examine what is possible in their own situation. If many teachers have been unsuccessful in demonstrating commitment combined with impartiality, there is no implication that another teacher must fail.

What would be involved in seeing that such attempts *are* unsuccessful? This is a complex matter calling for interpretation and judgment. If the students adopt the teacher's point of view, this may be simply the result of his or her position of authority. Equally, however, it may be because the arguments presented by the teacher were judged by the students to be convincing; or because their own reflection on the evidence and arguments led in the same direction. If the force of authority were at work, how lasting is this effect? Is it, perhaps, in time a stimulus to the student's own critical reflection on the issue in question? Clearly, there are difficult judgments involved here, such that confident pronouncements based on appeal to "research" are quite misleading.[60]

To what extent do we know that the teachers observed are those who, in general, manage to communicate that they take their students' ideas seriously? Identifying these would be no easy task, of course, but it would surely be a prelude to forming a representative sample. We might hypothesize that such teachers could state their own views and be seen as remaining open to criticism. I am not aware, however, that any serious attempts have been made to gauge the effectiveness of such teachers, nor to assess the performance of teachers who have become *sensitive* to their position of authority and who attempt to offset this influence.

It is hard to avoid the impression, despite appeals to what research is supposed to show, that philosophical assumptions encouraged the view that empirical confirmation was not required since we were really dealing with necessary truths. For example, non-neutrality was simply equated with promoting or propagating one's own view on the basis of authority. Being neutral was identified as being open-minded.[61] Such assumptions are not likely to incline anyone to ask how far a teacher who reveals his or her commitments is being open-minded, nor to help anyone to recognize open-minded teaching in practice.

The Humanities Curriculum Project tested its claims concerning procedural neutrality in the context of the controversial topic of racism. Earlier research in 1969 had indicated that attempts to promote racial tolerance through teaching might actually be counter-productive.[62] A study in 1971, however, based on six schools employing the strategy of procedural neutrality reported that "there was no general tendency towards intolerance after a seven to eight week teaching programme."[63] Stenhouse expressed the view that there was reason to believe that "some positive effects, modest though they might be, might accrue from teaching to adolescents in the area of race relations for from six weeks to one term. . . ."[64]

There are several points to note, however, before we accept even these very tentative research findings. First, it is admitted that the groups compared in the 1969 and 1971 studies were very different. The former group consisted of older students who were generally judged to be highly prejudiced. The latter group were younger, generally better educated, and holding less prejudiced attitudes. We cannot assume that the strategy of procedural neutrality would have been effective with the former group. Second, later studies which compared procedural neutrality with a non-neutral approach failed to find significant differences between them.[65] Both produced favorable attitudinal changes. Of course, there are many doubts about the reliability of such tests, but at least we have no basis in research for concluding that procedural neutrality is more effective than other strategies.

The Humanities Curriculum Project is an example of research into teaching where the numbers were never really there at all, but the impression was created that one had only to open one's eyes to discover the empirical confirmation. The confident, one might say arrogant, dismissal of objections was out of all proportion to the available evidence. This is not to say that the impressions gained in what was essentially qualitative research are of no value. No doubt the authority status of teachers is more dominant than we had imagined. Perhaps it is very much more difficult than anyone had realized for a teacher to reveal his or her views and succeed in fostering independent-mindedness among the students. These impressions ought to give the teacher pause. It is a pause, however, during which the teacher's intelligent judgment needs to be exercised, not surrendered to the fallible judgment of others.

Conclusion

What emerges from the preceding discussion is the indispensable element of *critical judgment* in teaching. First, teachers need to think seriously about the nature of their enterprise if they are to avoid impoverished accounts which only limit their view of what is possible. The ability to seize such possibilities, however, is not something which can be reduced to a formula. Second, it is necessary to escape the trap of ideological argument which attempts to portray ideals as spurious if the importance of principles such as respect, humility, and integrity is to be appreciated. The interpretation and translation of such ideals, however, demands intelligent reflection. Third, it is crucial that teachers become aware of certain phenomena and practices which can interfere with their ideals. Here research drawing on classroom observation is central. But such findings do not lend themselves to rule-like remedies. Conceptual, normative, and empirical awareness is necessary, but it needs to be transformed by critical judgment into something meaningful and relevant. In this connection, philosophical reflection is invaluable.

Notes

1. Robin Barrow, "Does the question 'What is education?' make sense?" *Educational Theory 33*, 3/4, 1983: 191-5.

2. Jacques Barzun, *Teacher in America,* Boston: Little, Brown, 1946: 4.

3. Robin Barrow, "Back to basics," in Gerald Bernbaum (ed.), *Schooling in Decline,* London: Macmillan, 1979: 202.

4. Brian Hendley, *Dewey, Russell, Whitehead: Philosophers as Educators*, Carbondale: Southern Illinois University Press, 1986: 5.

5. Etienne Gilson, "The ethics of higher studies," in Anton C. Pegis (ed.), *A Gilson Reader*, New York: Image Books, 1957. (Essay originally published, 1927.) For a similar point, see Max Black, *The Prevalence of Humbug,* Ithaca: Cornell University Press, 1983: 76.

6. R. S. Peters, *Ethics and Education,* London: George Allen and Unwin, 1966: 15.

7. John White, *The Aims of Education Restated,* London: Routledge and Kegan Paul, 1982: 5.

8. Plato, Meno 96A.

9. Immanuel Kant, *Critique of Pure Reason Book 2,* "Analytic of principles" (1781). A similar point occurs in David Hume, *Enquiry Concerning the Principles of Morals,* Section 4 (1751).

10. Barzun, op. cit., p. 32.

11. Glenn Tinder, *Political Thinking: The Perennial Questions*, 4th ed., Boston: Little, Brown, 1986: 2.

12. Barzun, op. cit., p. 9.

13. Many such claims are discussed in Donald Cochrane, "Why it is in your interest to have a clear concept of teaching," in Donald B. Cochrane and Martin Schiralli (eds.), *Philosophy of Education: Canadian Perspectives,* Don Mills: Collier Macmillan, 1982.

14. See, for example, Philip W. Jackson, *The Practice of Teaching,* New York: Teachers College Press, 1986: 104. And Gary D. Fenstermacher, "Philosophy of research on teaching," in Merlin C. Wittrock (ed.), *Handbook of Research on Teaching* 3rd. ed., New York: Macmillan, 1986: 40.

15. F. A. Siegler, "Comments," in John Walton and James Kuethe (eds.), *The Discipline of Education,* Madison: University of Wisconsin Press, 1963.

16. John Dewey, *Experience and Education,* op. cit.: 48.

17. The possibility of such consequences also shows the important connection between sincerity of purpose and assessment in teaching. See my paper, "The roles of teacher and critic," *Journal of General Education 22,* 1, 1970: 41-9. Reprinted in William Hare, *Controversies in Teaching,* London, Ont.: Althouse Press, 1985.

18. John Passmore, "On teaching to be critical," in R. S. Peters (ed.), *The Concept of Education,* London: Routledge and Kegan Paul, 1967: 202.

19. R. S. Peters, "What is an educational process?" in Peters (ed.), *The Concept of Education,* op. cit., pp. 11-12.

20. This is the famous, final remark in his *Ethics* (1677).

21. R. S. Peters, "What is an educational process?" op. cit., p. 12.

22. Alan R. White, *The Philosophy of Mind,* New York: Random House, 1967: 66-73.

23. B. O. Smith, "A concept of teaching," in C. J. B. Macmillan and Thomas W. Nelson (eds.), *Concepts of Teaching,* Chicago: Rand McNally, 1968: 13.

24. Jackson, op. cit., p. 90. See also Israel Scheffler, *The Language of Education,* Springfield: Charles C. Thomas, 1960: 57-8.

25. Fenstermacher, op. cit., p. 39. His claim here does not depend on, or relate to, the dispute in philosophy as to whether reasons can be causes.

26. Fenstermacher falls into error when he claims that without teachers we would not have the concept of student. This confuses an institutional sense with a general sense. His claim is true with respect to the notion of pupil, but not with respect to that of student. We can study on our own. See my paper, "The concept of study," *Saskatchewan Journal of Educational Research and Development 8,* 2, 1978: 40-6.

27. Since this discussion first appeared, I have been pleased to discover a causal account of teaching defended in Allen Pearson, *The Teacher,* New York: Routledge, 1989.

28. Educational philosophers tended to accept the sort of view set out in P. H. Nowell-Smith, *Ethics,* Harmondsworth: Penguin, 1954, ch. 1. See also Nowell-Smith's inaugural lecture, *Education in a University,* Leicester: Leicester University Press, 1958.

29. Ivan D. Illich, *Deschooling Society,* Harmondsworth: Penguin, 1973.

30. Rachel Sharp, *Knowledge, Ideology and the Politics of Schooling,* London: Routledge and Kegan Paul, 1980.

31. On this point, see Harvey Siegel, "Critical thinking as an educational right," in D. Moshman (ed.), *Children's Intellectual Rights,* San Fransisco: Jossey-Bass, 1986: 48. Also my *In Defence of Open-mindedness,* op. cit.: ch. 5.

32. Bertrand Russell, *Principles of Social Reconstruction,* London: Allen and Unwin, 1916: 147.

33. Plato, *Protagoras,* 314B.

34. See earlier, chapter 6, this volume.

35. Plato, *Protagoras,* 318A.

36. Plato, *Laches,* 190B.

37. See my *In Defence of Open-mindedness,* op. cit., p. 8. Also my "Humility as a virtue in teaching," *Journal of Philosophy of Education 26,* 2, 1992: 227-36.

38. John Dewey, "My pedagogic creed," reprinted in R. D. Archambault (ed.), *John Dewey on Education,* New York: Random House, 1964 (Originally published, 1897.)

39. John Dewey, *Democracy and Education,* New York: The Free Press, 1966. (Originally published, 1916.)

40. Siegel, "Critical thinking as an educational right," op. cit., p. 40.

41. John Dewey, *How We Think* New Edition, Boston: D. C. Heath, 1933: 56.

42. Israel Scheffler, *Reason and Teaching,* Indianapolis: Bobbs-Merrill, 1973: 67. Scheffler states in *The Language of Education* (1960, p. 60) that his concern is essentially to provide a descriptive definition of teaching, an account of the accepted meaning. I have myself argued that some examples seem to support the descriptive account (Hare, *Open- mindedness and Education,* op. cit., p. 83), yet others fail to

satisfy the criteria which Scheffler states. It seems clear that a normative element has been introduced.

43. See Russell, *Principles of Social Reconstruction,* op. cit., p. 152. Russell's views on education and teaching are discussed earlier in chapter 2.

44. David Sadker and Myra Sadker, "Is the O.K. classroom O.K.?" *Phi Delta Kappan,* January 1985: 358-61.

45. Donald C. Orlich et al., *Teaching Strategies: A Guide to Better Instruction* 2nd ed., Lexington: D. C. Heath, 1985: 171.

46. Meredith Gall comes closer than most with respect to this in her paper "The use of questions in teaching," *Review of Educational Research 40,* 5, 1970: 707-21.

47. Richard W. Moore, "Open-mindedness and proof," *School Science and Mathematics 82,* 6, 1982: 478-80. The point is discussed earlier in chapter 3.

48. A. N. Whitehead, *The Aims of Education,* New York: Mentor Books, 1949: 19 (Essay originally published, 1916.)

49. Robin Barrow has developed the most significant and thorough philosophical critique of research on teacher effectiveness in his *Giving Teaching Back to Teachers,* Brighton: Wheatsheaf, 1984.

50. Mary Budd Rowe, "Wait, wait, wait . . . . ," *School Science and Mathematics 78,* 1, 1978: 207-16.

51. Rowe, op. cit., p. 212.

52. John Dewey, "What psychology can do for the teacher," in Archambault, op. cit., p. 201 (Originally published, 1895.)

53. J. T. Dillon, "Alternatives to questioning," *High School Journal 62,* 5, 1979: 217-22.

54. J. T. Dillon, "Using questions to foil discussion," *Teaching and Teacher Education 1,* 2, 1985: 109-21.

55. Lawrence Stenhouse, "The humanities curriculum project: The rationale," *Theory Into Practice 10,* 3, 1971: 154-62.

56. Lawrence Stenhouse, "Controversial value issues in the classroom," in William G. Carr (ed.), *Values and the Curriculum,* Washington, D.C.: MEA Publications, 1970: 106.

57. Lawrence Stenhouse, "Neutrality as a criterion in teaching: The work of the Humanities Curriculum Project," in Monica Taylor (ed.), *Progress and Problems in Moral Education,* Windsor: NFER, 1975: 130.

58. Lawrence Stenhouse, *An Introduction to Curriculum Research and Development,* London: Heinemann, 1975: 118.

59. Stenhouse, "Controversial value issues in the classroom," op. cit., p. 106.

60. Sometimes described by others as "hard-nosed field experiments." See Paul R. Klohr, "A regeneration of the humanities," *Theory Into Practice 10,* 3, 1971: 147-8.

61. Lawrence Stenhouse, "Open-minded teaching," *New Society 24,* July, 1969.

62. H. J. Miller, "The effectiveness of teaching techniques for reducing colour prejudice," *Liberal Education 16,* 1969: 25-31.

63. Gajendra K. Verma and Barry MacDonald, "Teaching race in schools: Some effects on the attitudinal and sociometric patterns of adolescents," *Race 13,* 2, 1971: 187-202.

64. Stenhouse, *An Introduction to Curriculum Research and Development*, op. cit., p. 130.

65. Gajendra K. Verma and Christopher Bagley, "Measured changes in racial attitudes following the use of three different teaching methods," in Verma and Bagley (eds.), *Race, Education and Identity*, New York: St. Martin's Press, 1979.

9

Slogans In Teaching

Four fashionable ideas in educational theory are here identified as essentially amounting to slogans in which mere rhetoric supplants rational discussion. First, the back-to-basics movement, trading on a preference for what is essential and useful, disguises the point that there is serious dispute about what is actually essential in education. Second, progressive educators favor discovery learning, but ignore the fact that discoveries can grow out of teaching situations. Third, the idea of the hidden curriculum is used to denounce subtle indoctrination, but it is too readily assumed that a hidden curriculum is both inevitable and undesirable. Finally, modern educators have succumbed to the apparent security offered by behavioral objectives without noticing that many educational outcomes, including dispositions, cannot be specified with the precision demanded. Slogans offer simplistic solutions, and serve to curtail serious criticism.

Introduction

Many educational issues have come to be couched in the language of slogans, that is, catch-phrases which serve to provide a focus for a movement in education.[1] There are many other ways in which contemporary ideas could be approached, but slogans provide one useful way of identifying topics which are getting attention and stirring people. Of course, not all talk about education takes the form of slogans, but a good deal of it does and there is no reason to believe that slogans will be eradicated. They are not indeed always harmful, for they can call attention in an effective way to an educational problem or goal. We do, however, need to recognize them for what they are. If a slogan is effective, it changes the situation which made it necessary, and it may cease to be such an important idea to press for. The slogan, therefore, needs to be assessed in context. Again, if a slogan exaggerates for effect, there is a danger that other ideas may be ignored or unduly neglected. We must, therefore, ask about the merits of the ideas captured in the slogan, in order to avoid being persuaded by emotive language to take the slogan too literally. Let us turn immediately to an example.

Back to Basics

Teaching always involves teaching something to someone, but the range of things which can be taught is enormous. Hence, every curriculum represents a selection, and one of the fundamental questions in educational theory is how this selection is to be made. This was the problem addressed by Plato when he wondered how children are to be brought up, and also the problem which prompted Spencer's famous query: "What knowledge is of most worth?" The "back-to-basics" movement is one answer to this question.[2]

This slogan must be seen to some extent as a reaction to child-centered theories of education, which had their heyday in the late 1960s and early 1970s. The Hall-Dennis report[3] may be taken as typifying such an approach, with its emphasis on the child's interests and needs. Freedom and openness were very much in the air, and the traditional curriculum was judged to come off rather badly by these standards. Interest and variety were emphasized in the increasingly popular smorgasbord metaphor of the curriculum. But metaphors invite answer in kind, and there were many at hand to condemn the cafeteria curriculum. Here the suggestion was that any sense of a balanced and coherent curriculum had been abandoned.

If we view "back to basics" in this context, it is clear that it amounts to a plea to return to what is perceived to have been an earlier emphasis in curriculum. But what the basics are, which we are said to have lost sight of, is not made clear. What is meant by basic? We may approach this question by distinguishing three distinct, albeit related, aspects of the concept. (1) In one sense, the notion of what is basic refers to what must be learned first if other things are ever to be learned. A simple example is captured in the saying that we must learn to walk before we can run. Here the emphasis is on the more elementary. (2) In a second sense, the concept indicates that certain ideas are presupposed in others. Fractions, for example, presuppose the idea of whole numbers. In a logical way, whole numbers are more basic. (3) In a third sense, "basic" can suggest that which is essential, important, and central. Here we find what is thought to be basic contrasted with what is peripheral. Certainly, these senses overlap. One and the same thing may be judged to be basic, or fundamental, in each of these ways. But it is important to see that the uses drift apart in ways which make the slogan of limited value.

There are two main points to be noticed. First, in the things which we learn initially, that is, those basic in the first sense, many other matters are presupposed, that is, those basic in the second sense. For example, the number relations which are implicit in our elementary ability to count are not self-evident. Or to adapt an example from Aristotle, when we imitate the actions of people who are just, our actions presuppose the idea of justice which we, as children, do not yet understand. Second, the fact that something is learned first, or is required before further learning can occur, does not mean that it is somehow more important than other matters. There is no easy move from the first sense of basic to the third.

It would seem that the proponents of the slogan have mainly had the first sense in mind. In catering to the students' interests, the complaint is that the basic, elementary skills of reading, spelling, and arithmetic have been neglected. This is surely the point being made by those who claim that students are leaving school illiterate. A similar idea lies behind criticism of recent programs in values education. In encouraging students to discuss controversial topics, for example, it is alleged that the simple, traditional virtues have been undermined. Moral education was examined earlier in chapter 4, but the relevant point to note here is the demand for a return to familiar, trusted, and basic values.

In agreeing, however, that literacy, numeracy, and the traditional virtues are important, we must be careful not to frame our entire notion of what is educationally important in terms of these basic skills and values. To say that something is important is not to say that it is the *only* thing which is important. The point is obvious enough, and would hardly need to be made were it not for the fact that it seems to be ignored. There are two related errors here. First, elementary skills and traditional virtues have been identified as "what education is all about." Second, the fact that such skills and values are useful has led to the view that unless something is useful it cannot be important. The first mistake leads to a limited conception of education; the second to a limited conception of what is worthwhile. The result is a point of view that regards advanced study as superfluous and subjects such as art and music as ornamental.

Consider how different are the implications for education if "basic" is interpreted in sense (2) above. Here "back to basics" would entail an attempt to uncover the ideas which are implicit in the many things which we learn. For example, the "New Math" movement was concerned to change the situation in which children simply did not grasp the concepts which were presupposed in the drills and routines practised in elementary school. A new emphasis was placed on coming to understand the underlying concepts and principles. The same kind of emphasis has come to be seen as important in the teaching of other school subjects, and there is good reason to believe that this is a desirable development. Why?

In asking what is important or central in education, we need to ask what is presupposed in our very concept of education. In the language of the slogan: What is basic to the idea of education itself? It is clear, for example, that there is a conceptual difference between education and training. It is one thing to know how to do something, but a person with know-how will not automatically be said to be educated. Fundamental to the idea of an educated person is the matter of understanding principles, getting beyond mere rules of thumb. Secondly, the educated person is not one who is narrowly confined to a particular area of knowledge. Of course, it is not possible with a concept such as education to specify exactly what an educated person must know. To look for this kind of precision would not be appropriate.[4] But we expect to find some breadth of knowledge. Finally, we might notice the importance of certain attitudes in our concept of education. In particular, the educated person cannot be closed-minded, for this would suggest that he or she did not care to reflect on the beliefs held.

This is just the beginning of an analysis of the concept of education, but it is sufficient to show that the popular meaning of "back to basics" is hopelessly inadequate. The three Rs and the traditional virtues, important as they are, do not begin to meet the criteria of understanding, breadth, and open-mindedness built into the meaning of education. Nevertheless, to the extent that our schools really have neglected useful skills and basic values, the slogan serves a worthwhile purpose. It becomes counter-productive, though, if we start to interpret it as an adequate answer to the problem of curriculum selection. We need to remember also that our sense of what is valuable is not restricted to what is useful. Art and music may not be terribly useful judged by certain standards, but they have an intrinsic worth, which is valued for its own sake. There must be some things which are valued in this way for the following reason: Things which are valued because they are useful are valued because they lead to certain ends. But why are these ends valued? Clearly, some of these ends must be valued for their own sake, and not merely because they lead to other things, otherwise the chain of reasons would never be completed.

Discovery Learning

One of the ideas strongly emphasized in the educational reform movement of the 1960s was that of the student as an independent inquirer, finding things out his or her own way. This idea came to be captured in the slogan-like formulation "discovery learning."[5] Since, as we have seen above, there is now something of a backlash against "progressivism" (using that label in a suitably neutral way), it is important to think about discovery learning before we too quickly abandon what might, after all, prove to be a useful idea.

Let us be clear at once that the main ideas captured in this slogan are not at all new. These ideas include learning by experience, strategies of inquiry, being curious, and the use of equipment and apparatus. Discovery learning is not the name of one particular method, but of a whole family of ideas which stress the active involvement of the students. Such ideas can be found in Socrates, with his emphasis on dialogue; in Aristotle, with his concept of learning by doing; in Descartes, with his famous method of inquiry; in Rousseau, with his stress on the importance of Emile becoming able to go on acquiring knowledge on his own; and in Kilpatrick, with his activity-based curriculum leading to intelligent self-direction. These examples may serve to show that the ideas in question have a long and serious history.

It is not difficult to see why such ideas would be thought central by educational reformers. Discovery learning is an approach which serves to undermine authoritarianism in teaching, where ideas cannot be challenged and criticism is stifled. It also stands opposed to mindless rote learning and places an emphasis on understanding. Finally, it recognizes the creative potential of students and rejects the idea that learning is simply a matter of coming to know what others have discovered. These aspects of discovery learning are very clearly related to those fundamental features of the concept of education identified in the previous discussion of the basics. In particular, we can see at once a link with the point that an educated person has an understanding of principles, and also remains open-minded about ideas.

Difficulties arise, however, when these useful aspects are exaggerated. Of course, such exaggeration is sometimes necessary to achieve the desired effect of making people take notice. One task of philosophy, however, is to put these ideas into perspective, and this means being able to recognize exaggeration when we meet it. For example, one claim sometimes found is that students cannot understand something fully when they learn it from a teacher. They must find out themselves. This is the view that Descartes subscribed to in places.[6] There is, of course, a sense in which understanding does demand personal discovery, because in the end the student must come to see that such and such is the case for himself or herself. This logical truth, however, must be carefully distinguished from other claims. After all, a student may come to see the point as a result of good teaching. There is no warrant for the conclusion that the student must find out on his or her own. An explanation offered by someone else may be sufficient for a full and complete understanding.

Of course, there are certain things which we are likely to understand better if we have had personal experience of them as opposed to instruction about them.[7] My understanding of life in a concentration camp is unlikely to be as adequate as that of a survivor. This same example, however, shows that we cannot defend discovery learning in every case, since there are many experiences we will not allow our children to have. Obviously too, there are many experiences which we cannot have, for example the experience of being a member of another race, and yet it is equally clear that we can go a long way towards understanding such experiences through the accounts given by those who have had them, or through simulated cases. Any general claim to the effect that a man cannot understand what it is like to be a woman, or that a white person cannot understand what it is like to be black, invites the question: How could anyone know that this general claim is true? The claim implies an awareness of what men and white persons can understand, presumably held by women and persons of color, yet such awareness is precisely what the claim holds to be impossible. The point is that imaginative writers and resourceful teachers can get us to understand ideas which we may not have experienced personally, and which we did not work out for ourselves. We may take these ideas and develop them, but that does not mean that we could, or would, have arrived at those ideas unaided. Teaching and discovery learning are not in conflict, for discovery learning can occur in the context of teaching. It is one of the forms which teaching can take; experiences can be so structured that we learn what we would not have learned if left to our own devices. A further point is that teaching of a more direct and traditional kind need not militate against intelligent self-direction. Armed with certain basic skills and knowledge, students may continue as independent learners. Whether or not they do so will very much depend upon the spirit in which the early teaching was given.

"Discovery" has success built into it. I do not discover something unless I really succeed in coming to know it. This conceptual point is significant in two ways. First, we must not assume that simply setting up discovery lessons in our classrooms will guarantee success. The students may simply not see in certain pieces of equipment the underlying concepts, which are, of course, there to be seen. The camouflaged bird can indeed be seen in the trees, but only by the trained observer. Secondly, it follows that discovery learning, properly understood, is not open to the charge sometimes made that it abandons standards. Not every outcome counts as a discovery. Thus although one argument in favor of discovery is that students find such an approach more enjoyable and interesting, relevant standards must also be brought into play if the concept of discovery is to apply. If the concept is applied seriously, it is clear that it does not open the door to an undisciplined approach, where one idea is as good as the next and anything will count as worthwhile learning.

The Hidden Curriculum

We have seen that some educational theorists believe that the progressive movement of the 1960s went too far in the direction of freedom and openness in schools. At the same time, however, there are others who think that the reforms did not go far enough and that the changes were really superficial rather than fundamental. The basis of this charge can be understood if we bear in mind that certain strategies or approaches can contain or presuppose values. These values can be said to be hidden, that is, implicit rather than explicit. Even if attention is not drawn to these values, they may still be picked up by children if the values are part of the fabric of their activities and relationships. The importance of this in education was not lost on Aristotle. In recent years, however, the phenomenon of the hidden curriculum has been seen to have sinister overtones.[8]

Radical critics of schooling have pointed out that schools have a hidden curriculum. Beyond the overt curriculum, which teaches the various skills and values and ways of thinking deemed important, a further set of values and beliefs is being subtly reinforced. For example, children may come to believe that the only things worth learning are the things taught in school.[9] This translates into the belief that what is not included in the official curriculum is not important, or into the belief that students cannot decide for themselves what is significant. Moreover, they may come to look upon school subjects such as history and science as pre-packaged commodities for consumption, rather than living forms of inquiry to which they might be able to contribute. The teacher/student relationship itself may translate into an authority/deference relationship, in which students learn to be passive and to accept things on authority. This is reinforced by the fact that schooling is compulsory and creates a hierarchy of rights and duties. There may, in addition, be other hidden but clear messages, such as that certain subjects are more important than others, that certain subjects are only or more suitable for boys, or that competition is better than co-operation. The conclusion, in short, is that schools are by no means as open as we may have thought. The hidden curriculum poses an obvious threat to the notion of education, with its emphasis on critical thinking, understanding and open-mindedness.

It is foolish to deny that such a phenomenon exists, though we may properly question the alleged content of the hidden curriculum. This will doubtless vary from context to context, depending on the way in which certain activities and relationships are interpreted. Some critics, however, maintain that certain aspects of the hidden curriculum have always and everywhere been the same and will continue to be so as long as there is schooling. Ivan Illich, for example, has said this about the belief that only what is learned in school is important. Perhaps we can agree that there is always the possibility that such a belief will be formed. After all, if schools have the trappings of authority and wisdom, one may well conclude that the official curriculum contains the items which are worth knowing. There is no reason whatever to agree, however, that such an outcome is *inevitable*, though in fact we find this being claimed.

The first point to be made in rebuttal is that schools can attempt to bring the hidden curriculum into the open, and there is no reason in principle why such attempts must fail. Questions can be asked about the assumptions and presuppositions which lie behind the overt curriculum, and students can be encouraged to think critically about these. Secondly, teachers can try to ensure that their own behavior suggests that they recognize their own fallibility and limitations. Here the phenomenon is turned to advantage, because the teacher's behavior can suggest an attitude of inquiry and criticism. If it is true that messages can be implicit in what we do, as it surely is, then we can attempt by our actions to suggest educationally productive ideas.

There is no guarantee, of course, that we will succeed in eliminating undesirable ideas. We continue to be horrified by the examples of racism and sexism which we discover in school textbooks and which often were not consciously incorporated. We learn to read more critically and recognize prejudice where we once did not. There is no reason, however, to draw the pessimistic conclusion that teaching is inevitably tainted. If we discover and remove one example of racism, we make our work a little less prejudiced. If we wait until we can write the perfect textbook, we shall never begin at all.

The hidden curriculum is indeed an important and proper tool in education. There are many things, such as style and attitudes, which cannot be taught in a direct manner. They must be taught indirectly, usually by being shown or exemplified in practice. Often, they will be destroyed if self-consciously addressed, because this will introduce a false note. It will all seem unnatural and the students will be alienated. Some lessons must remain hidden, but this need not imply indoctrination. Students can, as we have seen, be encouraged to reflect critically on the values they are acquiring. The importance of such reflection could itself be part of the hidden curriculum of the particular school.

It is curious that the pessimistic conclusion should be frequently drawn, for it suggests the paradox of educational theorists who apparently believe that we cannot learn from our mistakes.

Behavioral Objectives

It is important to see the necessity of some form of assessment in teaching. Testing and grading have been under attack in the recent past, and certainly legitimate criticisms of particular forms of assessment can be made. Tests can be unfair in various ways, and grades are often inaccurate. We can be misled by test results into labeling students as failures or high-achievers, and find ourselves making a self-fulfilling prophecy. That is, we expect certain students to do well, and our positive attitude ensures that they do succeed. By contrast, the "dumb" ones never seem to learn. These real problems, however, do not justify the general conclusion that assessment *per se* must be abandoned.

In fact, assessment is logically required. To teach is to attempt to promote learning. The attempts may or may not be successful, the methods may or may not be suitable, the level may or may not be appropriate. If we are serious about our objective, however, then it follows that we must be concerned to discover if our efforts are on the right track. This means trying to ascertain if learning has occurred, and this clearly means that the students must somehow be assessed.

A second point can be made to support this view. In order to make intelligent plans for teaching, we need to know what our students already know. This is relevant in two ways. First, people cannot be taught what they already know. Secondly, we cannot decide on level or relevant content if we do not know where our students stand at present. Again, this means that they must be assessed. No particular form of assessment is implied, but some kind of assessment is necessary.

In recent years, a powerful demand has been made for a particular kind of assessment. It is said that tests must seek to identify behavioral objectives. In brief, the view is this: Teachers must have in mind, and students must be aware of, certain objectives or aims in the course or program, and these must be expressed in terms of specific behaviors. That is, at the appropriate time, the student must be able to do such and such. Of course, behavior must be construed broadly enough to include verbal behavior.

Apart from forcing teachers to think more seriously about what it is they are trying to achieve, the merit of this slogan is that it takes a stand against vagueness in educational aims. If the latter are not clear and precise, we can never be sure that they have been reached. The traditional faults of testing are only encouraged when objectives are stated vaguely. Assessment itself becomes subjective, impressionistic, and unfair. Why not state our aims in clear, unambiguous terms, so that it will be clear to all whether or not a student can do what is expected?

It is not necessary to oppose behavioral objectives altogether. It is important, however, to be aware of certain shortcomings. First, being able to perform in a certain way cannot ensure that the student understands. At the very least, we need to recognize the possibility that the student merely seems to understand. Of course, we can only gauge understanding by observing behavior – we have no access which is more direct. The point is, however, that another piece of behavior may indicate that the student does not really understand. Secondly, and conversely, we need to recognize that the student may indeed understand even without exhibiting the behaviors specified by the objectives.[10] Although all good teachers are aware of these points, they are in danger of being neglected in the enthusiastic endorsement of behavioral criteria. This leads to the dogmatic view that these, and only these, behaviors will count.

A further objection is this: There are certain important goals in education which cannot be adequately captured in terms of specific behaviors. For example, we surely want our students to develop certain dispositions and traits. We want them to read, go on inquiring, be honest, critical, and so on. This means that they have to develop certain tendencies, but tendencies are not all-or-nothing in nature. They are revealed in the sorts of ways in which people often behave in certain sorts of circumstances. This is much less precise than a limited set of specific behaviors, but not on that account hopelessly vague. Assessment here clearly calls for intelligent judgment rather than simply ascertaining the presence or absence of a particular behavior. We are in danger of ignoring important objectives if we limit our aims to those outcomes which are readily and precisely measurable.

We should continue to make our objectives as precise as we can, since there is no virtue in being vague for its own sake. Aristotle made the point, as we have seen, that it is a mark of the educated person not to expect the same degree of precision in every context. When we do formulate our objectives in precise, behavioral terms, we should remain open to the possibility that we may be ignoring other ways of demonstrating the ability in question. If we take seriously the goal of critical thinking, we must also remain open to the possibility that the prescribed objectives will be found wanting in some way. This is simply to say that it will be necessary for teachers to continue to exercise their own judgment. The important matter of assessment cannot be reduced to a purely mechanical affair.

Conclusion

The importance of judgment underlines the general danger of slogans. Slogans are often useful in drawing attention to a neglected point of view. But they also serve to interfere with our powers of independent and critical thinking. Issues are presented in over-simplified, black-and-white terms, and the appropriate qualifications and disclaimers are omitted. Analytical philosophy of the sort practised here provides a way of examining the ideas embedded in slogans.

Teachers need to develop the skills in question, for it seems likely that slogans will continue to characterize educational debate.

Notes

1. For relevant discussions in philosophy of education, see: B. P. Komisar and J. E. McClellan, "The logic of slogans," in B. O. Smith and R. H. Ennis (eds.), *Language and Concepts in Education*, Chicago: Rand McNally, 1961: 195-214. Also: Israel Scheffler, *The Language of Education*, Springfield, Ill.: Charles C. Thomas, 1960, ch. 2. And: Olivier Reboul, *Le Langage de l'Education*, Paris: Presses Universitaires de France, 1984, ch. 3.

2. For another discussion, see Robin Barrow, "Back to basics," in Gerald Bernbaum (ed.), *Schooling in Decline*, London: Macmillan, 1979: 182-232.

3. *Living and Learning*. (The Report of the Provincial Committee on Aims and Objectives of Education in the Schools of Ontario) Toronto: 1968.

4. cf. Aristotle, *Ethics Book 1*, ch. 3.

5. For an excellent discussion, see R. F. Dearden, "Instruction and learning by discovery," in R. S. Peters (ed.), *The Concept of Education*, London: Routledge and Kegan Paul, 1967: 135-55.

6. See Descartes, *Discourse on Method*, ch. 6.

7. This concession gives no support to the fashionable position that one cannot understand what one has not directly experienced.

8. For a recent discussion of the hidden curriculum, see John P. Portelli, "Exposing the hidden curriculum," in Sharon Bailin and John P. Portelli (eds.), *Reason and Values: New Essays in Philosophy of Education*, Calgary: Detselig, 1993.

9. See Ivan Illich, *Deschooling Society*, Harmondsworth: Penguin Books, 1973, ch. 3.

10. Fill-in-the-blank tests, which in some schools have virtually replaced the traditional essay, commonly fail here by recognising one and only one correct response.

10

Reading the *Apology* in School

Apart from those schools which have introduced the philosophy for children program developed by Matthew Lipman, the traditional school curriculum finds little room for philosophy. Occasionally, however, in the context of other subjects, a piece of philosophy will appear, such as Plato's *Apology* in an English reader. Such rare opportunities need to be seized by the teacher if students are to gain some sense of a subject by and large neglected in our schools.

Introduction

Writing in 1922, R. B. Appleton was able to dedicate his book on Greek philosophy to the sixth formers he had taught at the Perse School in Cambridge.[1] Appleton commented in the preface that he was convinced that elementary philosophy made an excellent school subject and he hoped that his own book would make a contribution to the teaching of philosophy in schools. He rather modestly added that he had written his book because he knew of no other "which treats the subject in a fashion simple enough to be understood by those whom I have had primarily in mind." Unfortunately, these hopes for the subject in school were not to be fulfilled; even classics, within which philosophy gained a slight foothold, has all but disappeared. Only occasionally do philosophical pieces turn up in the regular curriculum nowadays, one such example being Plato's *Apology* which continues to appear in texts of readings in English literature classes.[2] No doubt, it owes its place to the fact that it is rightly recognized as a great work of literature, full of drama, humor, and tragedy.

Doubts, however, about any proposal to make use of its appearance to introduce some philosophy in the school context may be anticipated. Is the *Apology*, after all, a suitable vehicle for exploring philosophy? The question here centres on how much philosophical interest there is in this work as distinct from literary appeal, or historical interest in someone who was a philosopher. It might be urged, for example, that the *Apology* is essentially a narrative and, unlike Plato's other works, does not pursue a particular philosophical problem. In any event, is the school a suitable place to begin philosophical inquiry? The worry here, no doubt, is that "teaching philosophy" might amount to little more than making superficial comments about philosophy, a result which would run counter to Socrates' own conception of philosophy as an *activity*.

The Philosophical Interest of the *Apology*

Students at university are often frustrated when their philosophy teacher cannot provide a succinct definition of the subject. It takes time to appreciate that any account of philosophy is bound to be controversial and that a definition of philosophy itself invites philosophical reflection. The *Apology* has some interesting reflections on the nature of philosophy which can stimulate class discussion. First, we receive a very powerful impression of the seriousness of philosophical inquiry. For Socrates, philosophy was a way of life which he was not prepared to abandon to save his life.[3] Philosophy, then, is not an idle set of intellectual puzzles but a way of thinking which affects our lives in a profound way. Second, the actual way of life practised by Socrates identifies philosophy with the careful search for truth through reasoned discussion and argument. Although Socrates refers to a prophetic voice which speaks to him, he is not in fact defending any sort of mystical approach to philosophy where the truth is somehow revealed in a special state of awareness. Truth has to be seen as such as the result of rational argument. These are views about the nature of philosophy which conflict with popular, stereotypical notions, and thus help to get students started thinking more seriously about philosophy.

In addition, however, the *Apology* contains a great number of philosophical themes which, although not pursued in great detail, have inspired subsequent philosophers to ask questions which might otherwise have been neglected. We may consider three examples:

1. First, there is the Socratic idea that we do not know as much as we think we do. It is, of course, attributed to Socrates that he said: "I know one thing, that I know nothing." This remark, out of context, might leave the impression that Socrates was a sceptic, like his contemporary Cratylus, believing that nothing is or can be known. Such an interpretation, however, would be a mistake. Socrates' view is that human knowledge is limited not non-existent. He does not deny, for example, that the poets and politicians have some knowledge. What they lack, he argues, is an appreciation of the fact that they do not know everything, and that their expertise is limited to a certain area. Moreover, Socrates shows that he believes it is important to go on seeking knowledge, a view which would be senseless if knowledge were impossible. Finally, he himself offers some ideas about what is true, as we will see, and thus cannot believe that truth is quite unattainable. Socrates leaves us with the question: What are the limits of human knowledge?

2. Second, we encounter the Socratic view of moral goodness and value.[4] He is concerned to make the point that we have our priorities confused. We set out to avoid death at all costs, forgetting that what is important is living a good life.[5] In the hope which he expresses for his children in his final words, Socrates again suggests that material possessions can distort our perception of what has value. The *Apology* draws our attention to import-

ant concepts like honor, justice, and moral commitment, and Socrates sets before us a new standard of moral ideals. The question arises: By what set of values should a human being live his or her life?

3. Third, the *Apology* introduces the idea of a society which permits rather than stifles criticism, even though in the end Socrates is put to death. This idea has inspired all those thinkers, including John Locke, John Stuart Mill, and Sir Karl Popper in our own day, who have attempted to defend an open society. Socrates compares himself to a stinging fly which is annoying but at least keeps the horse alert.[6] His point is that criticism and inquiry need to be tolerated, and we are forced to ask: How much liberty should a society permit?

It should be no surprise that the questions which arise in these three examples sound like an agenda for epistemology, ethics, and political philosophy, for Socrates is important in the way suggested by Bertrand Russell when he said that the value of philosophy lies as much in the questions which it raises as in the answers which it provides.[7]

Philosophical Problems in the *Apology*

If students can learn something about the general nature of philosophy and its main problems, the *Apology* also provides an opportunity to do some hard thinking about several puzzling remarks which Socrates makes. Indeed, students sometimes wonder how Socrates can be regarded as an important philosopher when he makes certain claims which seem obviously false. Here is an opportunity to drive home again the importance of critical reflection as opposed to learning what a philosopher has said. Again, let us consider three examples:

1. Nothing can harm a good person[8]

One's immediate inclination perhaps is to dismiss this as false and foolish. Good people are often harmed – they are injured or suffer serious illness. The problem of evil, that is, how God can be good and omnipotent and yet permit human suffering, would not be the problem it is if only the wicked suffered.

The first point to make by way of reply is that Socrates is proposing a new way of thinking about harm, much as Christ was to propose a new way of thinking of being someone's neighbor in the parable of the good Samaritan. The revised concept of harm has to do with moral damage to our characters, in a word, corruption. So we are not to think of every unpleasant outcome as a harm of any significance.

This clarification, however, may well prompt the charge that Socrates is inconsistent, for early in the *Apology* he insists that wicked people have a corrupting influence on others.[9] It is clear too from later remarks that Socrates views political life as potentially corrupting.[10] Even in the new sense of harm as moral corruption, it seems that good people *can* be harmed.

What is required at this point to show that Socrates is not contradicting himself is close attention to the nature of the claim that a good person cannot be harmed. It is clear that it has been wrongly taken as a kind of prediction or factual comment about what happens to good people, but it is a different sort of claim altogether. Socrates is making a purely conceptual point about what it is to *be* a good person. It is as if he were to say: As long as you remain a good person, it follows that you are not corrupted. The Greek makes this clear by saying essentially that there *is* no evil in the good person. It is, if you like, a logical truism, but it is not trivial. It brings out what is meant by the phrase "good person" and this is a notion which is controversial. Students can begin to appreciate how philosophy is concerned to explore and explain our concepts, to make clear what in a sense we already know.

2. Where a man has once taken up his stand . . . there I believe he is bound to remain[11]

Again, one may wonder how sensible this is. Taken literally as referring to a position in battle, is it not sometimes prudent to retreat in order to fight another day? Taken metaphorically, is it not stubborn and closed-minded to go on defending a belief past a certain point? Moreover, such an attitude surely sits uneasily with Socrates' general view that we should subject our beliefs to on-going critical examination.

The first point to notice in response is that Socrates is mainly thinking of those fundamental principles which we have settled on after much thought. Some of these are so important and basic that we may not even able to *imagine* circumstances in which they might be given up. A principle of this sort would be, for example, a prohibition against punishing an innocent person, a case which Socrates mentions when he reports that he was once ordered to arrest Leon of Salamis who was innocent.[12] (Incidentally, this case also shows that Socrates does *not* hold that orders must always be obeyed.) Certainly the circumstances would have to be very extraordinary before certain principles could ever be broken, and perhaps some are simply absolute. Secondly, Socrates is anxious to show that if a principle is given up in a particular case, the reasons which lead to this must be of a certain sort. In particular, we cannot allow personal inconvenience to enter into the calculation.

Socrates goes so far as to say that we must prefer death to dishonor, and this may strike us as an impossibly high standard. We need to remember, however, that Socrates is in part trying to delineate an ideal and, therefore, the fact that this sets out a demanding standard is no objection. Moreover, while we are no doubt sometimes prepared to excuse those who compromise their principles to save their own lives, there are other occasions in real life where we expect the highest standard. A person who betrays his or her friends to the enemy in order to save his or her own skin may be harshly condemned.

3. We are quite mistaken in supposing death to be an evil[13]

A cynical response would be that this is easy to say when one is seventy years old. Socrates himself seems to have been concerned about his own safety as a young man, since he gives as one reason for staying out of politics the fact that such involvement would have cost him his life.[14] Apart from the apparent inconsistency, is it not more reasonable to view death as a very great evil since it means the end of the only life we can be sure of?

There are a number of points to be made if this remark is to be properly appreciated. First, Socrates is not to be understood as belittling the value of life. There is no suggestion here of the existentialist view that life is meaningless and absurd, or that suicide is the only rational action. Notice that when Socrates says that political involvement would have cost him his life, he adds: "Without doing any good to you or myself."[15] Hence, it would have been a pointless waste, and such a death would have been an evil in as much as it would destroy the possibility of doing good. Second, Socrates is in part making the point noted above that every decision in life must not be based on the calculation of the risk of death. Third, of course, he is also rubbing in the point about the limits of human knowledge, for we do not really know what death holds in store. We are, therefore, pretending to know more than we do in claiming that it is evil. (Perhaps on this point, however, it might be retorted that Socrates likewise goes too far in saying that we are "quite mistaken" in calling death evil. His point should be that we cannot be quite certain that it *is* evil. Moreover, the fact that we do not know what it entails does not mean that we are wrong to fear it, since what we fear in this case is precisely the unknown.) A final point which Socrates has in mind is surely that there is an important sense in which the innocent person who is killed is not harmed as much as the one who murders him, a point we are likely to overlook if we think of death as the greatest evil.

These examples, raising as they do the concepts of corruption, moral principles and death, deal with issues which teenagers will surely find interesting and about which they will have their own views. They will begin to discover that the concepts in question are more complex than they appear at first sight, and that apparently paradoxical claims can begin to make more sense when carefully considered. In attempting to understand and criticize these claims and others, they will be approaching philosophy as a critical activity rather than as a collection of grand pronouncements.

It will emerge that, among other things, philosophy is concerned to draw careful distinctions, and to this end the *Apology* will provide them with many basic tools. Socrates begins by distinguishing rhetoric and truth, and proceeds to separate philosophy from sophistry. Belief is not the same as knowledge, and knowledge is different from wisdom. Students can start to explore the basis of these distinctions, and to apply them to their own studies. There is now a good deal of evidence that students can tackle philosophical issues much earlier than was once thought,[16] and it is a great misfortune that many students, perhaps most, leave school without ever coming to appreciate what philosophy is. It is unforgivable when the curriculum happens to contain in the *Apology* such a fertile ground for exploratory work. If some teachers can take the lead in redirecting attention to the philosophy of Socrates, students will once again become aware of the existence of a way of thinking which contemporary schooling virtually ignores.[17]

Notes

1. R. B. Appleton, *The Elements of Greek Philosophy*, London: Methuen, 1922.

2. One of my own children encountered it in grade 9.

3. Plato, *Apology* 29D. In Hugh Tredennick (trans.), *The Last Days of Socrates*, Harmondsworth: Penguin, 1969.

4. See also my discussion in "Socrates," *Ethics in Education 1*, 4, 1981: 6.

5. *Apology* 39A.

6. *Apology* 30E

7. Bertrand Russell, *The Problems of Philosophy*, London: Oxford University Press, 1912.

8. *Apology* 41D

9. *Apology* 25C

10. *Apology* 32D

11. *Apology* 28D

12. *Apology* 32C

13. *Apology* 40B

14. *Apology* 31E

15. *Apology* 31E

16. The evidence comes mainly from the work of Matthew Lipman and his associates at the Institute for the Advancement of Philosophy for Children, Montclair State College, New Jersey. There is now a video available about this work entitled *Socrates for Six year olds*, Princeton: Films for the Humanities and Sciences, 1991.

17. My discussion here is entirely elementary, intended only to suggest some possibilities to teachers who have an interest in philosophy. In preparation for a unit on Plato's *Apology*, teachers might profitably consult C. D. C. Reeve, *Socrates in the Apology*, Indianapolis: Hackett, 1989; Gregory Vlastos, "The paradox of Socrates," in Vlastos (ed.), *The Philosophy of Socrates*, New York: Anchor Books, 1971; and Thomas C. Brickhouse and Nicholas D. Smith, *Socrates on Trial*. Princeton: Princeton University Press, 1989. One valuable resource for the classroom itself is Gilbert Highet, "The trial of Socrates," a short talk available on cassette from Audio-Forum, Guildford, CT.